THE ART OF FAMILY LAW

Skills For Successful Practice

AUSTRALIA
LBC Information Services—Sydney

CANADA and USA
Carswell—Toronto

NEW ZEALAND
Brooker's—Auckland

SINGAPORE and MALAYSIA
Sweet & Maxwell Asia
Singapore and Kuala Lumpur

THE ART OF FAMILY LAW

Skills For Successful Practice

By

Anne Hall Dick

*Mediator and Specialist in Family Law Accredited
by the Law Society of Scotland*

and

Tom Ballantine

*Mediator and Specialist in Family Law Accredited
by the Law Society of Scotland*

EDINBURGH
W. GREEN/Sweet & Maxwell
2001

Published in 2001 by W. Green & Son Ltd
21 Alva Street
Edinburgh EH2 4PS

Printed in Great Britain by Athenaeum Press,
Gateshead, Tyne & Wear

No natural forests were destroyed to make this product;
Only farmed timber was used and replanted

A CIP catalogue record for this book is available from the British
Library

ISBN 0 414 013 719

PREFACE

"Where is the wisdom we have lost in knowledge?
Where is the knowledge we have lost in information?"
(T.S. Eliot, *The Rock* 1934, Pt I)

This book is written for family lawyers. Its aim is to help you not just to survive, but to enjoy, and hopefully excel in the family law field. The ways by which people can get advice and information are broadening and changing at a rapid pace. In particular with the advent of computer technology, clients are looking for more than just a professional "who knows the law"; they are looking for a whole further range of personal, analytical and management skills and qualities. This book is designed to examine those other skills and qualities. We aim to help you give three-dimensional advice taking into account legal, emotional and practical aspects.

What makes family law so different from other areas of law is the uniquely complex and intense interplay of the personal and legal. This makes it both interesting and challenging as a field to work in. Options are considered and decisions made on the basis of factors as variable and different as the people to whom they relate. Every client presents a unique combination of legal and emotional aspects. For each client you will have to find ways to create a workable pattern from the confusion of emotional and legal threads available. This makes huge demands on your ability to manage problem-solving processes and information while engaging and communicating with people.

It is extraordinary that, with the importance of the personal, there are innumerable books, lectures, articles at university and after about family law legislation and yet virtually none about managing the non-legal dynamics. We all have areas we need to work on to develop the three-dimensional thinking so essential in family law. We must make sense of people, law and practice. This book's aim is to provide new skills and a benchmark against which to measure your own approach. Much of what we say may reflect what you already do. We know that many of you will do some things differently and none the worse for that. The object is to explore and inform rather than prescribe. By making explicit what we think underlines much good family law practice we hope to take away some of the anxiety and stress for lawyers doing this work. We want to improve the delivery of legal services to those individuals confronting a family breakdown. We want family lawyers to enjoy a proper satisfaction from helping individuals who are going through times of change create workable, positive outcomes.

Family law is not as financially rewarding as many other areas of law. If practised with people skills as well as legal professionalism it delivers what few other occupations do—endless job satisfaction!

ACKNOWLEDGEMENT

First of all, a thank you to our own families, to Donna Ballantine and Peter Hayman for their support and encouragement.

In the course of our practice as family lawyers we have been inspired and helped by colleagues throughout Scotland. A heartfelt thank you to all of those who have been involved in FLA and CALM in general and in particular to those we roped in for specific input to this book: Liz McFarlane, Wendy Sheehan, Ewan Malcolm, Maggie Scanlan, Clare Craig and Lesley Anne Barnes.

Our business partners and colleagues at Anne Hall Dick & Co. and Mowat Dean WS have contributed tolerance, time and skills to take this project forward—a general thanks to all of them.

Thank you to Lynne Corrigan for her administrative work and to everyone at Greens for their valued guidance and input.

We also owe a huge debt to Lisa Parkinson who has provided us with a shining example of the benefits of combining intellectual and people skills, not only in mediation but also in all areas of life.

Solicitors south of the border have made an essential contribution; in the past through their help in setting up the Family Law Association and more recently through the valuable guidance of Dorothy Nott and David Hodson.

We have learned a great deal from all these people and hope we have managed to transmit some of their wisdom—any deficiencies in this book are all our own work!

Finally, to all family lawyers, may this book help you combine heart and head to enjoy a significant and valuable job.

CONTENTS

CHAPTER 2
PEOPLE SKILLS

CHAPTER 3
EFFECTIVE COMMUNICATION

CHAPTER 4
THE INITIAL MEETING

CHAPTER 5

METHODS OF DISPUTE RESOLUTION

CHAPTER 6

CREATING CHOICE

CHAPTER 7

ANALYTICAL SKILLS

CHAPTER 8
NEGOTIATION SKILLS

CHAPTER 9
CHILDREN

CHAPTER 10

MEDIATION

CHAPTER 11

MANAGING A FAMILY LAW TEAM

CHAPTER 1

INTRODUCTION

Why family law is important

> *"He's a human being and a terrible thing is*
> *happening to him so attention must be paid"*
> (Arthur Miller, *Death of a Salesman*)

If you considered what mattered most to you in life the chances are family (we use the word in its broadest sense) would come top of the list. Family relationships provide cohesion and meaning to most of our lives. Family law is important because it regulates this core part of our individual lives which also happens to be the building block of the wider community. It provides boundaries and benchmarks as protection and support at times which could otherwise be frighteningly chaotic.

Family lawyers make a difference

The failure of family relationships is devastating for those caught up in the fallout. When a family lawyer is invited by a client into his or her life to help them deal with the issues arising, it is both a privilege and a responsibility. It is a privilege because you are entrusted with something so significant to the individual. It is a responsibility because you can make a difference to material outcomes and ongoing relationships. People can either navigate the transition and move on to a different but positive future, or they can struggle against the current and end up with a future devoured with recriminations and bitterness over what has passed.

Those affected by family breakdown have available to them a surfeit of information through books, articles, friends, the Internet and numerous agencies. The real difficulty now is often not how to get information, but knowing how to use it. The legal knowledge we have is of course important but it is the way we sift, present and apply that knowledge, the way we interact with our clients and others, that will decide how good outcomes are, how well the individual's personal and material needs are met and

1

how far the individual members of the family survive and move on.

The value of maps

This book makes no reference to other legal texts. This may come as a relief but also reflects the dearth of material on what constitutes good practice for family law. We are stepping into territory that has been covered thousands of times over the years, with well-worn paths covering the terrain but with few maps made. Each of us will have taken an unnecessary diversion, confronted an extra obstacle, simply because we had no map to check our route against. Some of the paths we take might be downright dangerous for us or for our clients! Our aim is to map our view of what constitutes good practice. Other people would no doubt map a different and equally valid route. We do not believe there is or can be a definitive route. We do believe family lawyers should think about and always be looking for ways to improve on the individual route they take.

Themes to this book

A considerable source of anxiety for practitioners is the lack of guidance as to what constitutes good practice. Any attempt to set out a view as to what is good practice will have to presuppose some values which are not themselves demonstrably "right". This book is no exception. We want to introduce you to the values behind this book at the start. We provide more detailed guidance on how to reflect those values in your work later on.

Balance

> *"I do not admire the excess of a virtue like courage unless I see at the same time an excess of the opposite virtue as in Epaminandas, who possessed extreme courage and extreme kindness. We show greatness not by being at one extreme but by touching both at once and occupying all the space in between"*   (Pascal, *Pensees*)

Much of what constitutes good practice in family law is a question of finding a balance in using a wide range of skills. Different situations require different skills and approaches. None of us can claim to have every virtue but we can try to develop our skills to their full potential. The art is to have the broadest range of skills available to meet situations and the understanding to find the right balance in their application.

Know why you are doing what you are doing

A personal understanding of the values and intentions behind what we do is an essential base on which good practice can be built and against which it can be tested. Such an understanding also alerts us to when inappropriate personal views and biases are intruding on what we do. Our work and communication is value laden through our language and presentation whether we like it or not. The important thing is to make sure the values are appropriate and consistently applied.

All parties in family disputes are to be respected

When we act for a family law client we only hear one side of the story. There is a natural temptation to see the "other party" in a negative light because of what our client has told us. We resist this and remind ourselves that there are always two sides to a story because it happens to be true. However, there are occasions when, even knowing both sides of the story, we feel precious little sympathy for one of the protagonists (cases of domestic violence spring to mind). It is very rewarding to work for a client we perceive as decent, friendly, and conciliatory. It is more difficult to work for someone who is bitter and vengeful.

The reality is that clients and their partners are the products of infinitely complex influences. Their behaviour will be affected by both recent and distant events. We need to respect that complexity and avoid judgement. This is not an invitation to ignore or accept the unacceptable. It does not require us to like both parties. It does require us, while pursuing our client's interests assertively, still to extend professional courtesy and respect to our client and the other party through their agent. "Demonising" a protagonist artificially limits our understanding and therefore our ability to find options that would meet each parties appropriate interests and thus provide a solution.

It is unhelpful for professional advisers to become attached to their own client's version of events or to their own client and to identify their client as "right" or "wrong".

Clients need to feel safe

While parties need to be respected your client also needs to feel safe. Clients need to feel sufficiently secure and trusting in their relationship with you that they are able to disclose intimate and embarrassing information—domestic violence in relationships is underreported to legal advisers. Where a disclosure of this sort takes place, it should be treated with the utmost sensitivity and seriousness. On these occasions swift and assertive legal remedies are to be encouraged.

Clients should be helped to find their own solutions

Family lawyers cannot provide a diagnosis and select a remedy for relationship ills. They can, and should, ascertain issues to be resolved, the information necessary and options available to resolve them. A theme of this book is that it is the client—properly supported and possessed of a clear picture of the benefits and disadvantages of options available—who chooses. He or she finds the point at which he or she can assent to an outcome on the range from the rigid application of legal criteria to the distinctly unusual, legally unorthodox but personally satisfactory resolution. This is not an easy way out for family lawyers. It is usually far more of a challenge to really explain and truly explore the reality of various possibilities, to listen attentively and respond appropriately rather than briskly sum up the options analytically and provide your "answer".

Fairness and reasonableness are key guiding motifs in legislation and court procedure to achieve justice in family actions

We have gone out of our way, as far as possible, not to relate this book to any specifics of legislation or procedure. In mapping our idea of good practice we have attempted to keep our perspective on justice at the broadest possible level. With the important exception of the child related issues, where the welfare of children has to be the dominant motif, we perceive the achievement of fair and reasonable solutions by fair and reasonable means as at the core of our judicial system. We accept that what we mean by fair and reasonable is subject to continuing evolution and change.

Clients should be encouraged to give a proper emphasis to the needs of children

The law gives the best interests of children a paramount importance in decisions affecting them. The law cannot ensure that what carers do outside court reflects that importance. When acting for adult clients and not their child or children, we can recognise that very few parents would say they want other than what is best for their child even where their actions suggest otherwise. We can help them to act in accordance with what they say. It is within our professional remit to encourage clients to consider the needs of children at all stages in negotiations and reflect their importance in solutions reached. Gently helping adult clients turn their thoughts from a short to a long term view of a situation can help parents function better in the present and have more chance of well balanced offspring in the future.

Separating couples have much in common

It is ironic that at a time of division, separating couples have much in common, although they may be at different points in their acceptance of the separation. They can feel hostility towards each other as husband and wife or ex-partners while still acknowledging that they both need a house and food and want the best possible arrangements for their children. If the starting point for a client is a desire for retribution and the extraction of at least a pound of flesh the outcomes are unlikely to be satisfactory, may take a long, costly time and will not necessarily bear out the maxim that "revenge is a dessert best eaten cold".

If a client can reach the point of accepting their goals should be the best available outcome in line with the law, with the least possible damage to the children, satisfactory outcomes are more likely to be achievable.

A theme we develop is that the family lawyer's task is to acknowledge and deal with the negative emotions that get in the way of resolution and to engage the client in the more positive task of finding the best available outcome. For a client the uncomfortable truth to be accepted is that short of a judicial decision, which may satisfy no one, an acceptable solution to his or her housing, income, relationship needs is only likely to be achieved if his or her partner believes he or she has attained a similarly acceptable outcome.

Conciliatory but assertive approaches work best

There is a wide range of views on the approaches to be encouraged in family law. Survey after survey has illustrated the destructive effect on children of continuing confrontation between carers after separation. The implication from that is sometimes taken to be that court should be avoided at all costs. Court is usually not desirable but if, for instance, a father believes contact with his or her child is in that child's best interest, delay in seeking contact through the courts, where other avenues might be preferred, can be crucial to whether contact is restored or not.

This book promotes conciliatory but assertive approaches to problems. It is not a contradiction to be conciliatory in tone while at the same time, where appropriate, indicating time scales outwith which a judicial decision will be sought. What is best for a child may sometimes actually be better achieved by a quick restoration of contact through a court decision rather than a long conciliatory but fruitless dialogue.

The theme of conciliation attaches to other issues too. If a couple can sort out financial matters by a co-operative approach the emotional fallout can be lessened. That does not mean that there are no occasions when immediate, tough action needs to be taken. If assets are being moved or financial support is not being given, quick action may be essential. The distinction is between assertive but conciliatory representation which is desirable and aggression which is not. The former involves a proper balancing of the legal and personal arguments and a reasoned presentation, the latter implies an attempt to gain an advantage by posturing and emotional overlay. The delineation is not always clear cut because, on occasion, you will have no alternative but to take a strong stance which can be perceived as aggressive. The distinction can be as much in how you present things as what you present.

The way a solicitor relates to and represents a client can and usually will affect the way parties relate to each other and deal with their problems

> "Tolerance and justice, fearlessness and pride, reverence and pity, are learned in a course on long division if the teacher has those qualities"
> (William Alexander Percy, *Lanterns on the Levee*)

An important element of mediation is the modelling by the mediator of behaviour he or she hopes to elicit from a couple at mediation. A thread running through this book is that the same applies to a lawyer's approach to family work. If the lawyer takes on and buys into a client's way of looking at the situation, the client has the best possible validation of his anger, hatred, or other strong emotion. If a professional adviser is angry, abrupt or emotional in his or her communications with a client or other agencies, there is little encouragement for the client to adopt a different approach.

An additional offshoot of inapt behaviour, in particular towards an opposing solicitor, is the real possibility that the other party will identify you with your client and direct anger towards you as well as his or her ex-partner.

The distinction is again between assertive co-operation where possible, assertive action where not, as against hostility and an inappropriate aggressive overlay.

Court-based outcomes should not brutalise!

Family lawyers tend to spend most of their time advising and negotiating but where court action is the appropriate way forward it should be approached with courtesy and competence. The skills outlined in this book can be applied to achieve effective but humane outcomes.

Systematic methods of addressing family issues are helpful

We suggest systematic approaches because the issues involved can be so diffuse and intermingled. To give some sort of structure allows the client to get an idea of what to expect and gives you a framework within which to operate. If the innumerable byways of family law are leading astray there is a steadying point to return to. We offer structures in the understanding that systems are not always workable, not appropriate to every case and will be given a different emphasis by different people.

We recognise that the appropriate timing of steps taken within any structure is important in achieving satisfactory outcomes, both emotionally and financially for the client.

*Family law support staff are a vital part of delivering a good
service to clients*

Careful thought and attention needs to be given to how consistent
courtesy and competence can be achieved from the moment a
client walks through the front door for the first time to the
moment they leave through it for the last time.

Boundaries

*Family Lawyers should recognise and act within their skill
boundaries*

In dealing with families, solicitors are sometimes expected to
be amongst other things doctor, counsellor, psychologist,
judge. Some of the skills you have to use are analogous to
those professions. However, it is vital to identify your
professional boundaries and to not move from expressing
appropriate non-expert knowledge and support into giving what
purports to be advice when such advice can only be provided by
an expert.

Not a doctor

You can and should keep an eye on how your client appears to be.
There is a spectrum of mental states along which we are all
placed. Where a particular trait crosses over into being a medical
condition is not something we are qualified to decide. If there are
concerns about a client's mental or physical health they should be
advised to see their doctor or, if relevant, an expert opinion
should be obtained. If you have doubts about your client's ability
to give instructions, with your client's permission, an expert
opinion should be obtained.

No definitive statement can be made of when an expert's
involvement should be sought but it is better to err on the side of
caution.

Not a counsellor

You should of course be sympathetic but cannot take on the role
of counsellor or psychologist trying to sort out what may be
difficult, non legal, emotional or psychological issues.

The recognition, acknowledgement and accommodation of emotional and psychological issues are necessary and appropriate. The in depth analysis and treatment of symptoms arising from those issues are beyond your boundary however much you may want to treat them. An attentive recognition of strong emotion can be a powerful release of blocks to problem solving. If blocks remain more specialised help can be suggested tactfully.

Not a judge

Over and over again, clients will try and draw us into an emotional involvement in their view. He or she will want you to make a judgement on his or her spouse. We should not be drawn in. We are there to provide objective advice on the basis of the evidence in front of us and in the knowledge that there is someone else somewhere else quite probably giving a diametrically opposite view of the situation and attempting to elicit the same emotional involvement from their representative. Again, that does not mean be unsympathetic, simply retain your objectivity.

Solicitors require and deserve respect and consideration too

It is surprising how often in our concern for our client and to meet our professional obligations we forget that we are human beings too! Boundaries do not just apply to skills; they also apply to solicitor/client relationships and expectations. Precisely because relationship issues matter so much to clients what they want from you can extend well beyond what they are entitled to expect. Family work can be stressful at the best of times. Solicitors are entitled to respect and appropriate treatment by clients just as much as clients are entitled to the same thing from us.

A theme that permeates this book is that your client's personal problem is your professional problem and the distinction should not be blurred.

Our approach to this book

We have tried to offer this book in the most logical way possible moving through foundation points for the work to key skills and finally more particular special areas of concern. Many of the illustrations refer to married couples because it is briefer but when we talk about family relationships we are talking about all the myriad forms these may take including unmarried and gay relationships.

Conclusion

Managing facts and feelings in an integrated and constructive way is the key to appropriate outcomes whether from advice, negotiation or litigation— knowledge of "black letter" law is assumed. This book aims to guide you through relevant

- people skills
- thinking skills
- organisational skills

to allow you to make that knowledge work creatively for your clients and rewardingly for you.

- Values colour everything we do
- All parties in family disputes are to be respected
- Clients can be helped to find their own solution
- A proper emphasis should be given to the needs of children
- Conciliatory but assertive approaches work best
- Work within your skill boundaries
- You deserve respect and consideration too

CHAPTER 2

PEOPLE SKILLS

"The universe is transformation; our life is what our thoughts make it"
(Marcus Aurelius, *Meditations*, Book 11, Chap. 5)

Introduction

Family law clients are in the throes of profound life changes. Whether these have been triggered by your client, or his or her partner, the consequence for both is a state of uncertainty with endless practical tasks to be tackled.

Dealing with tired and over-stretched clients can be tiring and over-stretching for legal advisers. The way to avoid that destructive loop is to recognise that factual information is not enough. Facts are helpful in tackling issues to be resolved, but not the complete answer when emotions are a strong driving force. Constructive problem solving involves both logic and emotion; it is a creative and practical process. Facts alone will not deliver a workable formula for the future. Feelings need to be harnessed to facts in a positive way to move things forward.

If you ignore the emotional signals from your client, he or she is likely to feel misunderstood and defensive. If you respond appropriately to the emotional messages, you allow your client to relax and gain access to information and the possibility of sorting things out.

This can be done without a crash course in psychology. What is needed is for you to pay enough attention to the client to allow the client in turn to be able to pay attention to you.

Paying proper attention should spring quite naturally from having a kindly curiosity in what is going on for your client with a view to working out how your knowledge might be of assistance. There are specific skills which can be used to give that attention more focus—

- **acknowledgement** allows emotions to be identified and released

11

- **normalising** enables a client to regain confidence and feel less isolated
- **clarifying** demonstrates interest and avoids misunderstanding
- **summarising** helps make information digestible and keeps planning on track
- **mutualising** uncovers areas of common ground
- **reframing** provides an opportunity to help your client start seeing solutions, rather than remaining stuck in problems

These are skills which are much used in mediation. Although it is useful to look at them in turn, it is also important to recognise that they are all facets of understanding, rather than manipulating your client. If strong emotions go unacknowledged, then so may any information you dispense to your client. Denial of emotions is liable to go hand in hand with denial of facts. Acceptance of one promotes acceptance of the other and represents the first step towards dealing with rather than denial of change.

Acknowledgement

All change, even positive change, is stressful. It can seem very threatening. Fear inhibits problem solving. It tends to put people in either fight or flight mode. It impedes objective assessment. Small problems can seem disasters. Big problems can seem like the end of the world. Strong emotions are triggered. The first step in neutralising the negative impact of emotion is simply to acknowledge it. Unacknowledged, the underlying energy is either dissipated in panic or bursts out in anger. Once acknowledged, the energy can be used to sort things out.

> "... when a strong emotion wells up in us, or a
> powerful mood takes us over ... the head becomes a
> slave to the heart" (Dylan Evans, *Emotion*,
> Oxford University Press, 2001, p.112)

Since the heart is in turn enslaved by the emotion, the way to catch the client's attention is to start from that focal point. You can reach your client by recognising the emotion which is absorbing him or her. If you do that in a sympathetic and neutral way, it creates the opportunity for dialogue which can start allowing both heart and head to function again. The way you do this is crucial. If your recognition comes across as siding with the client, you will just reinforce the grip of the emotion. If you ignore the emotion, you and your client will be trying to communicate in different languages with mutual incomprehension the likely result. You may each shout louder in your own language. Your rational logic may become more strident and the client's emotional state more florid.

Acknowledgement need not be elaborate. Good timing and simple language are key factors. It is usually good to do some initial acknowledgement. A client telling you about separation, or possible separation, or problems in their family, probably needs to hear you say something like:

- what a lot to cope with
- it sounds like it's quite a frightening time for you
- it seems like a confusing situation

The right phrase will be dictated by the client's visible level of upset but your response must be authentic. You have to show a recognition of the other person's feelings, which cannot be applied mechanically. There must be genuine interest and a will to put your skills at the client's disposal. If someone is very upset, it is likely to be necessary to acknowledge frequently.

If the emotion is strong, your client may start crying. Offer a box of tissues and apologise for the fact that they are having to talk about such difficult things. It is often helpful once your client is a bit more composed, to offer to move on to some fact-finding to see what information might be of help. Your client may feel ready to provide information. That can be the bridge to processing information from you.

Remember acknowledgement does not mean taking sides. It is not buying in to your client's interpretation of what has happened and why. It is simply giving recognition to how they feel.

If a client announces within the first few moments that she will not let her husband see their children since he's gone off with someone else, hang on to your dissertation on joint parental rights and responsibilities until a bit later in the interview. Instead, recognise that your client is feeling hurt and scared. Comment that it sounds as if it's a difficult time for her and the children. Say you hope you'll be able to give her information that might help her make the right decisions and start asking questions about his circumstances. Give some practical information. Emphasise her importance to the children. Then start working your way round to thinking things through for the children and explaining the legal situation.

If another client announces that since his wife's decided she doesn't want to live with him, she can forget about getting any money from him, don't immediately deluge him with hard facts and number crunching. Appreciate his fear and anger. Say it sounds like he's been faced with big unexpected changes he didn't choose. Comment that he might be worried that more unwelcome things might happen. Mention that knowing the legal rules might help him plan things better and from that point go into explanation mode.

A sympathetic smile at the right time can do more for someone than a dissertation on financial advantage/disadvantage! On the other hand, sympathy should not be an alternative to knowledge. Clients need and are entitled to both.

Bear in mind that anger and fear are very close. It can be quite unnerving dealing with a client who is very angry. There is a risk it will put you into fight or flight mode. You might try to fend off the anger by reasoned argument and find yourself in a rather bad tempered exchange with your client. You might retreat into submission and find you have become the client's ally in anger rather than objective adviser. The best course is to recognise the existence of the anger first to yourself and then to your client. Recognise out loud that the situation sounds very frustrating, upsetting or distressing and that you'd like to see if information about the legal framework might help a bit can release a client from being stuck in fear or anger.

Normalising

This is also useful. If clients can be reassured that something they are experiencing is a normal even if unwelcome stage they will feel less isolated and therefore less defensive. It's very important to avoid being patronising or appearing to endorse the unacceptable. If a client is very upset by his or her children showing signs of distress after a separation it is important to agree that children will normally want their parents to stay together and grieve if they part but also mention that if the separation is carefully handled children can still cope. A comment that it is normal for people to feel hi-jacked by emotion for a while after a separation may provide relief for a client who feels scared by the power and unpredictability of their emotional roller coaster.

Other appropriate phrases might be:

- people usually feel overwhelmed when they have to tackle a lot of changes
- knowing what possibilities there are usually helps make things look more manageable

A helpful transition to information gathering at the appropriate time is to say something like: "Things must seem very unsettled for you. Probably the most helpful thing I could do is to ask you for some information. That will let me outline how the legal framework affects you. It will give you a better idea of what your choices are."

Never overlook the need to acknowledge. Sometimes a client may seem very composed at the first meeting. It could be at a later meeting that you hit some emotional rocks. Some clients may be really well adjusted and only fleeting acknowledgement would be appropriate. If at any point you begin to feel frustrated or impatient with a client make that a signal to check if you've missed a cue to acknowledge some strong emotion.

Clarifying

This is another important step in communication. If there is any doubt or ambiguity about any factual or emotional information you are picking up from the client, it is important to stop and check, rather than run the risk of false interpretations or misunderstanding. That can then lead into:

Summarising

As the exchange of information develops, it is important to summarise the ground you believe has been covered. It helps the client absorb and retain the information and ensures that both of you know what has been discussed and what is to happen next. The last two steps give you the opportunity to check that you and the client are both remaining on the same wavelength. If when summarising, your client nods energetically in response, you know things are on track. If your client looks doubtful or uneasy, then you have either lost the emotional pulse, or misunderstood some facts along the way. It is a sign of the need to rewind.

Mutualising

This allows forays into the common ground where solutions tend to be found. It involves recognising where objectives and anxieties are shared. This must be done with care. A partner who feels wronged may find it totally objectionable to accept that there are any such shared concerns. If sufficient acknowledging and reframing are done, it should be possible to take opportunities to point out shared themes. Be guided by remembering that both parents are likely to want things to turn out all right for the children, both partners will feel a sense of loss for what they hoped the relationship would become and everyone concerned is likely to be anxious about having somewhere reasonable to live and enough to live on. If you can use a combination of people skills to reach the stage of recognising these as a shared starting point, then the factual information can be used to explore possibilities.

Reframing

This involves taking a negative statement, recognising a positive and valid concern contained in it and re-stating the concern in a positive way. A client will often say what he or she doesn't want. Reframing is a helpful method of encouraging them to express what they do want. By doing this the client starts visualising something positive for the future rather than dwelling on negative aspects of the past.

When this is done successfully it operates on many levels. It creates a future focus making solutions easier to find. The climate becomes more problem solving than blaming and judgmental.

Great care is needed to ensure that the re-frame is an accurate reflection of the original underlying message. You should specifically check that point if the general response from the client, whether verbal or by body language, leaves any doubt.

One client might say "I want to make sure that she doesn't get her hands on my business." You could re-frame by answering "It sounds as if it is very important for you to safeguard your business as a going concern. There are a number of ways that could be tackled."

Another client might say "It's just not working letting the children see their father, they're upset and behave badly when they come back". You could respond "So you would like any contact between the children and their dad to work as a benefit for the children. Perhaps we could look at why problems sometimes crop up and how they might be sorted out."

Reframing can be a bridge from the past to the future, from negative to positive. It sows a seed of problem solving in acknowledgement. Timing is very important. When people are experiencing very high emotion they will tend to need their acknowledgement neat! If reframing is tried too soon or too clumsily it will come across as either confrontational or patronising or both. Done at the right time it can be like a magic wand.

Information gathering

People skills must still be put to good use when taking factual information from clients. What are straightforward facts to you may trigger fears or sorrow in the client. Keep an eye on your client. Be ready to acknowledge or normalise. Emphasise the information is to help you both look at possibilities. Clients may be furiously speculating why you want to know particular details. Explain the more information you have, the more possible choices you should be able to outline. At each meeting check if there have been any developments and mentally double check the possible implications of any changes. Think in three dimensions: emotional, practical and legal.

Continuous assessment

Remember that facts and feelings are interwoven, rather than in sequence. Keep alert to how your client is dealing with the situation.

If the client is very subdued and/or tearful he or she may still be overwhelmed by grief and loss. If they don't know much about the finances, they may have been used to being excluded from information and decision-making. Either way, it may be difficult for them to process factual information. Remember that does not mean they are unintelligent, just that they may need some further help to get into a problem solving mode.

If it has come across that the client has some very fixed ideas about what the law should be, and you know the legal rules are liable to disappoint, be on the alert for how the explanations are given. Recognise there is a risk that the information may be rejected or distorted. Take particular care to check the client has understood. Avoid appearing unhelpful by making it clear that whether or not the law is right in this case you know the client wants you to explain things properly without letting sympathy get in the way.

At this stage, you are working out how to ensure that your knowledge will unleash the energy of solutions, rather than be sucked into the vortex of despair, anger or justification.

Legal information

Research was carried out into written agreements and published in 1997: "Mutual Consent: Written Agreements In Family Law", F. Wasoff, A. McGuckin and L. Edwards (Scottish Office Home Department, Central Research Unit, 1997). Parties who had entered agreements some years before were asked for their views. Many were critical of the advice given to them by solicitors. A telling comment in the report is that: "A solicitor who took a relatively neutral stance and who outlined the options available and advised on the long-term implications of certain decisions was preferable but rarely encountered".

The more experienced you become, the greater is the risk that your increasingly wide knowledge will become completely inaccessible to the client. A specialist has been defined as someone who knows more and more about less and less. It is easy to lose touch with what it is like to know nothing about the subject. On the other hand, if you do not feel confident in your subject, you may feel nervous at being pinned down. Either way, the client may leave the office with little workable knowledge. We should take a lesson from the research, and combine people skills with knowledge, to provide relevant impartial information in the form of alternative possibilities and then potential consequences.

Check client understanding

It is not enough to give the correct information to a client; you must ensure that the client has taken it on board. Many articulate and intelligent clients would find it difficult to admit they have not understood what has been said. If you have been explaining some of the intricacies of financial provision, it is likely that many fellow lawyers might have found it difficult to follow! Clients who are tired or depressed (or both) may not have the energy to clarify things they found unclear. It is important to avoid appearing patronising when you check if you have gone over things properly. It can be helpful to make a habit of pausing from time to time and asking:

- this is quite a complicated area; does what I've said make sense?
- even if you think the rules are wrong, have I explained them clearly enough?
- I wonder if that explanation was rather muddled; could you let me know what it meant to you?
- we've covered a lot of ground today; would you like me to go back over anything?

Even if you are glancing down at your notes maintain enough eye contact with the client to detect panic. Catching a fleeting glance of incomprehension can help avoid the start of some profound misunderstanding that could shipwreck future discussion. Make it very clear that you would anticipate questions and clarification being necessary. Avoid a client feeling that they would appear stupid or impertinent if they interrupt your outpouring of erudition!

Promote problem solving

Encourage creative problem solving by fostering a future focus, stimulating flexibility and putting facts to good use.

Future focus

Initially, much of a client's energy may be devoted to trying to make sense of what has happened. They may have few mental and emotional resources left for future planning. If the client's focus is on showing his or her partner is in the wrong, or at least that the client is not at fault (or at the very least, not completely at fault!) it will be very difficult to look at realistic options for the way forward. There will be a tendency for the client to look for ways to emphasise the blame of the other person in any settlement possibilities or contact arrangements. There may be resistance to the concept of fairness or co-operation as parents.

It can be helpful to explain that the people who decide the legal rules recognised that the reasons relationships stop working are usually rather complicated. Although one person may be more at fault than the other, it can be difficult to disentangle just what went wrong. Rather than spend a lot of effort on analysing the reason for the breakdown it seemed more helpful to focus on making provision clear for the future to try to allow people to move past a difficult period in their lives.

Often much of the anger springs from grief at the loss of hopes and dreams about the relationship. It can help to acknowledge that and say:

- it can be very sad to think of how you hoped things would be
- it may seem like a terrible waste

then strike a more positive note by commenting that you probably had good times together in the past and you don't need to lose that

If clients do seem stuck in a groove of trying to make sense of things by putting the other person in the wrong, try asking the client if he or she thinks the other person will accept it was their fault. Usually the response will be an emphatic "no". You can then ask if it might be better for the client to devote their energy to put things right for their own present and future. Clients are often very responsive to moving onto a more constructive track if given a nudge in the right direction. It is important to give a nudge rather than a push! If you try using logic and law to shove clients along you are likely to find equal and opposite resistance from them.

Asking questions can be much more powerful than giving advice, no matter how sensible. You can ask your client if things have reached the point of no return in the relationship where it may be better to simply "agree to disagree" about how that happened. The client can acknowledge in turn to their partner that they just each see things differently. There is no need for either to "sell" their version to the other person.

Once the client is released into more objectivity it is easier to start looking at options. Solutions lie in the future, not the past.

Flexibility

Encourage clients to expand their range of possibilities. The more choices they are willing to look at, the more likely it is that they will find an acceptable outcome. If they have arrived with a very firm idea as to what should happen next, it is better to avoid either agreeing disagreeing. Instead, accept that as one option. Outline the pros and cons. If it strikes you as unworkable, give the client the information you have which makes you doubtful. Suggest having a look at other ideas. Brainstorm (see Chapter 6). Help the client assess their needs for the future realistically. Bring the factual information centre stage.

Facts

Facts can do quite a lot of the work in problem-solving if you have done adequate groundwork in acknowledging and information gathering and giving. Possible solutions start emerging from the legal and factual framework. You should not have to persuade your client about what do next. The facts should tell their own story. If you find yourself at loggerheads with a client it suggests that you:

- have too much of an investment in a particular outcome!
- have not sufficiently clarified the facts or the law
- need to do more acknowledgement before carrying on with the problem solving

General considerations

Courtesy and competence should be watchwords throughout. Professionalism alone will not provide the dynamic nor kindness the catalyst for change. Both are necessary. Individuals can demonstrate amazing courage and resource in facing difficult situations. They can often retain or recover a healthy sense of humour given half a chance. Insensitivity in a professional adviser can trample those positive qualities underfoot. Sometimes lawyers are nervous about how far to stray into the territory of interpersonal skills. They believe their knowledge of the "black letter" law is their strength and are rightly cautious to avoid anything resembling counselling. It is important and necessary to stay within boundaries. For family lawyers, the ability to make their knowledge accessible and usable must come within these boundaries.

Harnessing legal and interpersonal skills for a client's benefit can be exhilarating! The combination should allow your work to be fascinating and rewarding. Sometimes it will be the very opposite. There will be days when you feel drained. They should be the exception rather than the rule.

Conclusion

- You need sympathy as well as legal knowledge
- Remember to acknowledge and reframe
- Make the law relevant and understandable
- Create a problem-solving climate
- Check that the client understands

Further reading

Daniel Goleman, *Emotional Intelligence* (Bloomsbury)
    ISBN 0-7475-2830-6

Dylan Evans, *Emotion—The Science of Sentiment* (OUP)
    ISBN 0-19-285433-X

Stone, Patton & Heen, *Difficult Conversations* (Michael
    Joseph)
    ISBN 0-7181-4361-2

Maister, Green & Galford, *The Trusted Adviser* (Free Press)
    ISBN 0-7432-0414 X

CHAPTER 3

EFFECTIVE COMMUNICATION

"'When I use a word', Humpty Dumpty said in rather
a scornful tone, 'it means just what I choose it to
mean — neither more nor less'."
(Lewis Carroll, *Through the Looking-Glass*
(and What Alice Found There))

Language is important

It is rather obvious to say it but, of all the things used as a lawyer, the most important thing we have is words. It is surprising that no direct training is given to lawyers in the use of language. What we say and how we say it has a profound effect at various levels especially for family law clients. The right words chosen at the right time can help a couple move forward. The inappropriate word at the wrong moment can set off a chain of emotional or litigation fireworks.

The first thing to remember about words is that they have different resonances for different people. The sentence "James is sensitive" for one person might conjure up an image of a caring and responsive individual, for another someone excitable, easily wounded and yet another a highly perceptive man. All these meanings, come within the dictionary definition but the person hearing the words gives them his or her own particular colour.

Professor Neil McCormick of Edinburgh University Law Faculty delivered a riveting lecture on interpretation. During the lecture a young woman ran into the theatre and harangued Professor McCormick over his failure to meet her at a particular location for lunch. The students were all aghast at this unwanted interruption. Professor McCormick was a well-known Scottish National party supporter. Students, when asked what the altercation might be connected to, divided into three camps:

- something to do with politics
- something to do with the law faculty
- a romance

It turned out that the woman was an actress and the incident had been set up as a class exercise. What was interesting was not so much the categories that came up but the fact that, generally speaking, the individual's perception of what they had observed reflected their own personal interests. In family law events are particularly open to misunderstanding and misrepresentation due to the coloured perceptions of those involved.

Because of these difficulties when a client speaks to us there is considerable scope for misunderstanding. The language used is weighted with a whole history of personal associations. Physical abuse over many years may have been reduced to "arguments" in your client's lexicon of language. The victim, whose self esteem is shattered and world view warped, has adapted his or her vocabulary and downgraded the significance of the behaviour. If you took the client's word at face value instead of looking behind the word to find out what events it described, you would be none the wiser.

Lawyers cannot be expected to produce endless literary exemplars of absolute tact but they can be expected to think about what they say and the impact it will have on the people they are working with. They can also check the descriptive terms used by clients against the factual history to which they relate.

Certain basic elements mark out good expression in family law cases.

Accuracy

Accuracy is not just a matter of avoiding typographical errors such as a reference in a recent letter from a rather douce firm of city solicitors to the "erotic attendance" of a party for contact (wrong, but admittedly more captivating than the intended wording!). It is about thinking through the meaning and impact of all the words we use.

Keep it concise

Short simple sentences tend to work better for client understanding. Numbered points and short paragraphs also make for a clearer verbal picture.

Pitch it at the right level

In family law you are engaged in a constant struggle to communicate simply and yet accurately. Before starting a letter or meeting you should be thinking about your client and your assessment of their ability to understand what you have to communicate. That does not mean patronising people but rather acknowledging that some legal concepts are difficult to understand especially at times of stress. You need to find language appropriate to the particular client to express these concepts. If you are giving a broad picture, and not including the finer details, say so. Before using any legal term of art consider whether it is really necessary and if not, do not use it. If you must use it, explain what it means. Most categories of words can have their own particular unwanted resonances. Even a noun, without any qualifying adjective or other descriptive words, can still be devastating. The man who has struck his child and is termed an "abuser" receives all the baggage associated with that term.

Use adverbs and adjectives with care

Because adverbs and adjectives set out to communicate the qualities of verbs and nouns the dangers tend to be more obvious. Words to be used with care are "sometimes", "always", "never", "usually", "regularly", "frequently", and the like.

The misuse of words like "always" has prolonged the bitterness of many a family dispute. A client, two or three years after separation, nurtured a huge sense of anger because a writ for divorce included the sentence "He was always abusive to Mrs Jones when he came home after work". Mr Jones was furious. He acknowledged that "on occasion" he had been abusive and close questioning confirmed that by this he meant at most once or twice a week. Clarification through correspondence with the wife's solicitor suggested that this was indeed the case. The client believed that his wife had deliberately misrepresented the position to help her get a divorce. The client was assured that it was the solicitor who had not clarified meaning and as a result mistakenly overstated matters. The client still refused to accept his wife had not lied. He thought the solicitors were trying to cover up for her. You can argue that this individual had lost his sense of perspective. The answer is that, of course, he has. Many clients do at separation! Many clients are desperate to put the weight of failure on to their spouse rather than to carry it themselves. It is often easier to feel angry with "that liar" than to acknowledge "my mistakes". Sloppy use of language can seem trivial in itself but can have enormous repercussions.

To give another example, for a client to say "I've seen Mr Smith regularly with James" does not communicate anything much at all. How often is regularly? Does it mean that when the person occasionally saw Mr Smith, James was regularly with him? It is perfectly possible to clarify meaning by specific questioning. "How often do you mean by regularly?" If no clear answer is provided offer possibilities "once a week, twice a week, the last Friday of the month?". You can at least narrow the statement to give it in its clearest numerical form. Numbers provide accuracy and objectivity.

Another trait to be avoided is the over use of "very", "extremely" and the like. "Our client is extremely upset at this behaviour".

It may be that your client is upset in which case fair enough but there is a suspicion that if solicitors engage in an upward spiral of competing extremes which do not reflect reality and communicate an escalating emotional tone, if that tone wasn't there between a couple in the first place, it will develop as a result of the solicitor's use of language. What's more, the overworked words begin to lose their value. Once you've used "very" a few hundred times you've nowhere else to go but presumably "fantastically" or "very, very".

Adjectives too can be a source of unnecessary conflict. A "huge fight" occurred when your client failed to deliver the clothes. On this occasion the noun and the adjective are incorrect if what actually happened was that there was a short, muted argument on the doorstep.

It is not that adjectives and adverbs should never be used, it is that they should be used accurately and not overused. Most importantly you should consider whether their inclusion will be of any benefit to your client or simply feed the ever available fire of exaggerated and destructive allegation and counter allegation.

Do not overstate advice

In giving advice to clients the usual rule is that if you state things too emphatically or too specifically when the subject cannot bear that interpretation you end up embarrassed at best or with a misrepresentation at worst. There's no need to put yourself in that position. Advice is usually better conservative and qualified where appropriate by an "about" or "approximately". It is often accurate to say a particular settlement falls within the range of disposals a court would have, in your view, made but less likely to be accurate to say something is the "best" or "worst" a client can do. The occasion you use the overegged epithet will be the occasion, for some inexplicable reason, you are proved woefully wrong.

Be positive

Being clear, accurate and avoiding excessive expectations does not mean being negative. On the contrary the client generally benefits from realistic reassurances where they can be given. If you have given your client a picture of what the options and possibilities are they want to know that you can assist them to a workable solution to their problem.

In general, it is better, where possible, to point out the positive, rather than accuse of the negative, in addressing concerns of your client in talking with the solicitor of his or her partner. ("Our client would appreciate it if Sam could be sent for contact in his new gym shoes" is more likely to achieve a result than "Tell your client to stop sending Sam over in his smelly old trainers".)

Be objective

One of the least attractive forms of solicitors' correspondence still to be found is the type that states as fact what is actually a report from the solicitor's client to the solicitor. Do not underestimate the enormous power a typed letter on a solicitor's notepaper has for may people. It can appear to transform a thought or possibility into fact. Take a letter saying:

> "Your client appeared at our client's house on the 22 January 2000 and verbally abused our client. The police were called and your client was forcibly removed."

If this correspondence is based on a report from the client to the solicitor alone, it is irresponsible legal practice to present it as fact. If the solicitor spoke to the police who advised that they removed forcibly the other party it is appropriate to indicate that is where the information came from. There are several reasons why it is unhelpful to report a client's version of events as fact:

- You put yourself in place of the judge when you haven't got the evidence to do so and when that is not your job.
- If your client is lying, you yourself are, in plain English, lying.

- Your own client has been bolstered by a "solicitor's letter" presenting his version of events as fact. He or she may begin to view it as fact even if it is not.
- Other people who see the correspondence will assume it is fact.
- You are seen to be lacking objectivity.
- The client on the other side may increasingly direct his or her vitriol against you.

An accurate statement of the facts on this occasion would be:

> "Mr Smith advises us that Mrs Smith appeared at his house on the 22 January 2000 and was verbally abusive to him. We are told the police were called and Mrs Smith was forcibly removed. We have checked matters with the police who advise that they attended a domestic incident at the house and forcibly removed your client."

The statement will no doubt still be unpalatable to the other party but it has the benefit of being accurate. It implicitly recognises that there may be an alternative version of events.

Restraint

Do not overstate or colour your narration of events. It is very difficult when faced by a tearful client not to become engaged in their anger or anxiety to the extent your correspondence becomes charged in a way that helps no one.

Be assertive when required

Restraint is not an argument against assertiveness. It is perfectly sound to continue your letter after the incident of 22 January 2000 by saying:

> "Mr Smith wants relations between him and Mrs Smith to be kept on an amicable footing if possible in the interest of James. However, we have advised him that the behaviour he describes is inappropriate and that he should raise interdict proceedings if there is any repetition."

The position for Mr Smith is firmly stated. The responsibility for the protective measures is deliberately given to the acting solicitor to highlight the fact that there is a professional adviser recommending a course of action, it is not Mr Smith reacting inappropriately to a set of events. The aim is to communicate a position without adding unnecessary heat to the discussions between the Smiths.

The more unrestrained version (which we have no doubt all seen) might read:

> "Your client came to our client's house. Your client opened the door and called our client a 'fat cow'. Our client has no intention of taking this abuse from your client and he has told us to get an interdict if it happens again."

The statement is unnecessarily coloured, gives unnecessary details (*e.g.* we do not need to know precisely what was said), doesn't give necessary details (*e.g.* when is it supposed to have happened).

There is an argument that the more colourful version will have a more satisfying effect on the receiving solicitor. However, there is a distinct possibility that, with a similarly unrestrained receiving solicitor on the other side, it will open the way to even more correspondence about whether the conversation took place at the door or in the sitting-room and whether the words used were "fat pig" or "big sod".

If the client sees this letter it is inviting back an emotional, coloured response focusing on irrelevant detail. If that is how the correspondence between solicitors is going you can be pretty sure that communication between the clients will continue, or start to go the same way.

Much of the sense of the attitude of the other party a client gets is through solicitors correspondence. It may be the only contact he or she has. Your letters are an opportunity to model a different more appropriate way of talking. Because it is in print it is more powerful than speech in capturing and encouraging that different approach.

Forms of Questions

The way you formulate your questions has a huge impact on the information you obtain. A lot of the time we do not think about how we frame our questions and then wonder why we get more or less information than we wanted or the wrong information altogether. There are some forms of question that we all use without necessarily considering why we use them or whether they are in the right form for the particular objective.

Open questions

"Tell me what happened?"; "How are the children?"; "What do you want?". These questions invite a general response. They have their place, particularly at the start of acting for client, in giving you a context and information for more specific questions. They can be used to help a client elaborate on a particular point and often elicit feelings as well as facts. However if you are at a stage where you want to home in on a particular point the question form has to change. If you have a client who has little sense of proportion or of relevance you may well find that open questions lead to long unproductive interviews.

Closed questions

"What happened on the evening of Tuesday 21st April?"; "Which school does Gemma go to?"; "How often did he shout at you?". These questions are an effective method of control for you. They limit the information you get back. They emphasise facts. They can allow you to bring a structure to the meeting. They give you a precision that you will need for a writ. They avoid you getting an overstated or understated "word picture" of your client's situation. Sometimes you need to be prepared to follow one closed question by another:

Q. "How often did he shout at you?"
A. "All the time."

Q. "How often is all the time?"
A. "I don't know that I could say."

Q. "Was it once a day, once a week, once a month? Give me your nearest approximation."
A. "Probably about once a week."

Be prepared to spend the time needed to get accurate answers. Remember that if not used sensitively and with a leavening of more open questions your client could feel as if they are being interrogated. It is a question of balance.

Hypothetical questions

"If your husband were to leave the house would you want to buy it?"; "If your wife agreed to sell the house what amount of capital would you be prepared to give her from the proceeds?". These types of questions are useful at many stages. They are particularly useful when you are considering options. They allow you to "reality test" possibilities with your client while signalling, in the way that the question is formulated, that you do not expect your client to commit to the hypothetical situation

Circular questions

"What would Darren (client's son) say if you were to ask him to split his time 50/50 between you?"; "What do you think your husband would say if we asked him what was most important to him?" These are questions that invite your client to consider how another person is thinking. These question forms are useful in helping your client identify the mutual concerns, and possible ways of meeting their partners interests that will in turn make their partner more amenable to meeting your client's interests. They are useful in encouraging a client to shift his or her perspective and see things from the angle of their partner or child.

Leading questions

"Did he batter you when he got home?"; "Did he tell the children to call you a cow?". We all know that these are questions that suggest the answer we expect within the body of the question. Apart from in Court we do not always consider whether we should or should not be using them. As in court there are non-controversial areas where it is a waste of time and artificial to avoid leading questions. However on points of importance where you are establishing facts important to your clients position you should avoid leading your client and potential witnesses. You will not be able to do so if matters are dealt with in court and you might get a different answer to a differently formulated question. If you do lead you may give a suggestion of what you want that your client will happily store away and subtly incorporate into any further description they give of the relevant events.

"Devils advocate" questions

"Why is it better for Darren to live with you when he has been with his mother for the last 18 months?"; "Why do you think a court is going to accept your suggestion over that from a child psychologist instructed to provide an independent view?". The simple mechanism of confronting your client with the strongest elements of the opposite case can do wonders for a client's sense of realism. To preserve a working relationship with your client it may be useful to precede these questions with a health warning! Say you know your client is relying on you to think through things from all angles. Suggest you run through some challenges which could be made. Ask your client what response he or she could suggest. You can follow up your initial questions with circular questions putting your client in the position of a judge. If your client suggests that the child psychologist is biased, you might ask: "if you were the judge would you be likely to accept that an independent child psychologist would risk his or her professional reputation for a relative stranger."

Talking about children

What is best for the children

It is surprising how often a long letter or meeting about children can pass without any mention of what is in the best interests of those children. Talk is all about what the adult client or his or her spouse "wants", "will take", "will accept". It would be artificial to pretend that these things do not matter but the more the dialogue is framed in these terms the greater the potential is for conflict and the less chance there is for a proper emphasis on cooperation in achieving what is best for that particular child.

Mutual interests

What a couple should, and often do, want is what is best for their children. This is a shared goal, an area where you have the perfect opportunity to stress mutual interests (even if your client is not always consistent in expressing it as a mutual goal to you!).

It is both helpful and an accurate reflection of the law to bring clients back to the need to clarify what is best for the children. Your choice of words is extremely important in achieving that end. To say:

> "Your client has been telling James that our client is an evil man. Please make sure your client knows James should not be involved in the difficulties between our clients. If your client's behaviour continues in this way our client does not want James to have any contact with her",

might be an accurate statement of your client's sentiments but hardly helps move things on. Before writing anything it is worth considering with your client the effect on James of reporting what James said. If the comments are to be mentioned a different wording could model a different approach more in line with the law and the goal of an appropriate arrangement for James.

> "Mr Smith tells us that on the 16th January 2000 James mentioned his mother said bad things about Mr Smith to him. We have stressed to Mr Smith the need to encourage James' contact with his mother and to avoid involving him in the difficulties between our clients. If James is involved in this way we will have no alternative but to discuss with Mr Smith whether contact with Mrs Smith remains in the best interest of James."

Looking at the first sentence of each version on these occasions precisely what was said does not need to be repeated; the fact that it was negative is what matters. It is important to pin down a date for when the comment is supposed to have been made as, without that, individual incidents can get lost in a morass of allegation and counter allegation.

In the second version, second sentence there is a positive point about encouragement. Instead of telling the solicitor how to do his job it is drawing the other solicitor into the co-operative role of stressing what is inappropriate. It is getting the same message across as the first version but in a more palatable way. The last sentence firmly focuses the discussion on the mutual goal of James best interests not what the clients want.

The conscious or unconscious desire of parties to hurt each other by whatever means available, including through children, should not be underestimated. If the signal given is that by insisting on a particular type of contact the client is thwarting what the other party wants he or she may well seek to insist. If the message given is that James best interests will be affected the response might be different.

A child has a name

A final point on children is that they have names. If you refer to "the child" or "the said child" you are depersonalising and encouraging the treatment of the child as object or worse still prize. A name conjures up a face and a human being. The child's name should be used as far as possible.

Communicating with expert witnesses

There is an understandable desire to get experts say what you want to hear. The letter asking the question:

> "please confirm the injuries sustained by my client as a result of the assault by her husband"

might produce, to the instructing solicitor, a highly satisfactory response but the language is transparently leading and the response may well not provide the information you really need. A more circumspect approach may take more time but will give a more the accurate answer:

> We need to know if a client attended the doctor and if so when and for what reason.

> If the client has sustained injuries we want to know the likely cause of those injuries.

> We need to know the basis on which the doctor has reached a particular conclusion.

The terminology used by experts can be particularly confusing. Never be afraid to ask for definitions. Words which have one meaning in layman's terms may have a different meeting in a professional context. Make sure your client has some understanding of meaning too.

In thinking about an expert's communication, consider:

> First, what values lie behind the view expressed. Are they backed up by research? What tells him these values are meritorious?

> Secondly, the data on which a view is based and whether this data can support it. How often did he see the child? What was the venue? What are his reported observations of the child?

> Thirdly, whatever the conclusion does it follow logically from the data provided? If it is concluded that a child is scared of his father does the given data support that conclusion? If a business is valued at £500,000 does the data justify that conclusion?

Pitch/speed/tone/intonation/body language

Pitch and speed

Much of what we have said in this chapter relates to written communication but is equally applicable to how we talk. As well as what you say how you say it will have a substantial impact on your effectiveness. You will be surprised how often a client picks up on and starts to reflect what you do. If you are conscious of it happening you can make subtle adjustments to try and control the mood and tempo of communication. For instance the lower the pitch and the slower the delivery, within common sense limits, the more you can bring a state of calm to an agitated client.

Intonation/tone

If you speak in a warm voice with balanced, modulated phrases you have a head start in enabling a balanced, rational discussion. If you are tempted to convey anxiety, anger or other negative emotion you should be considering whether it helps or hinders your client.

Body language

You are hopefully not the type to thump the table or strike the forehead (at least until after your meetings with family law clients!) However in subtle ways a mood can be set. Leaning forward intently may show you are interested but can make some people feel crowded and intruded on and lead to a claming up. Leaning right back can give the message that you are thinking about the next game of golf and just want this rather distasteful person out of here. Equally, for some people, it can give a sense of space to talk. As always you need to watch and adjust your behaviour to suit the individual.

You need to watch your client's positioning too. The client who sits a distance away from you down the table may be a distance away from understanding what is going on! The client leaning forward nervously with their coat still on may be terrified of you, your office and his wife!

Eye contact

The term active listening may sound like a contradiction but with the wrong tone, body language and lack of eye contact you can give the impression of being mentally removed if physically present. Maintaining a soft involved eye contact with the client along with the right tone and body language lets your client know that you are attending properly to what is said.

Telephone language

Most of us spend a lot of time on the phone to clients and other solicitors. Being able to manage this is a particular skill. Many of us find it easier to be direct on the phone, to let our true views/emotions show through. Be particularly careful not to let your language move from the highest standards you have set yourself. To help you do this it can sometimes be helpful to try to visualise the person as in the room with you.

Silence

Do not be afraid of silence where a client may be about to disclose/decide something important. If your question has been properly and clearly stated be prepared to give space for an answer. If you need an answer to a particular question be prepared to repeat it.

Talking too much

If you are talking all the time you are almost certainly doing something wrong! Make sure you do not dominate exchanges and bulldoze through your client's voiced concerns and questions.

Be yourself

It may sound a bit rich to give this as a final point after all we have said! However it is the most important point of all. Most of us have a wide range of ways we express ourselves. The aim is to think about where you pitch your expression within your own range in an attempt to touch the bases mentioned in your own way. Most people can detect a false expression a mile off. You still have to be genuine.

Conclusion

- Use precise, clear language
- Be restrained and objective
- Always focus on the best interests of children in talking about them
- Stress mutual goals and concerns
- Pitch, speed, tone, intonation, body language can all help communication

CHAPTER 4

THE INITIAL MEETING

*"The meeting of two personalities is like the contact
of two chemical substances: if there is any reaction,
both are transformed"*

Carl Gustav Jung, *Modern Man
in Search of a Soul*, 1933

Introduction

Family breakdown affects the individuals involved. Advising
those individuals affects the solicitors involved. The movement
tends to be towards either understanding or self-justification. The
momentum gathers from the initial meeting.

What the client needs

The first meeting with a client needs special care. Initial meetings
with family law clients may become, for you, a daily task for
which you have a fairly predictable set pattern. An initial
interview for your client is likely to be a first such interview and
possibly one of the more terrifying events in their life. The
interview for you is likely to provoke sympathy rather than shock
or condemnation but for your client may be a source of acute
embarrassment, an acknowledgement of failure in a crucial part
of their life, a time when their private grief is exposed. We have
already discussed the importance of dealing with feelings and
communication skills. In this chapter we are going to address
requirements specific to a first meeting with a client. We
approach it on the basis that the client you are meeting is
considering separating from a married partner.

Reassurance

It may be the first time this person has been inside a lawyer's
office; even if it is not, he or she is going to share with you, a
total stranger, intimate details of his or her personal relationships.
The sharing is taking place at a time of difficulty and, quite

probably, extreme unhappiness. It is important for your client to know you are the right person to be doing the sharing with. Reassurance comes from you employing all the skills, organisation and knowledge you have at your disposal.

Sympathy

You can use all the right words, ask all the right questions, communicate all the right information but, if you are unsympathetic, you can guarantee your client will leave the meeting unsure as to whether they have the right solicitor.

Confidence

A client wants to know that you care, know your stuff, understand their problems, and will provide options to resolve those problems.

Knowledge

The client is there to learn what the law is, how it affects them, and what the options are for the future.

You need to know the essentials of the law as well as having an idea as to the potential short and long term dangers of and solutions to the client's situation.

Non-judgemental

Your client wants someone who is not going to judge him or her or the situation that has led them to seek advice.

Involvement

There can be an understandable desire on the part of solicitors to take control of the client's situation. Questions are asked, information given and the client told what to do. Some clients will want you to do this. The Scottish Law Society's *Better Client Care* Practice Management Manual states that "It is not unreasonable nor is it bad practice for a solicitor to give positive advice, taking care at the same time not to domineer". It refers to the creeping tendency in the profession to give a list of alternatives and say to the client "It is up to you". This matter needs to be addressed with care because of the parts of family work that have nothing to do with the law. Clients, for instance, weigh up the emotional cost against the psychological cost in deciding how far to pursue a favourable financial settlement. Clients try to decide what is in the best interests of children where judges in the highest courts often appear to have significantly different starting viewpoints on matters such as how far the law should go in allowing a father contact with his children. In our view if the client is appropriately involved in the process he or she can and should make his or her own decisions with you making the possibilities and advantages and disadvantages of those possibilities clear to your client. If you think the client is making a bad decision you can explain, kindly and clearly, the disadvantages of what they are proposing to do. This is you doing your job. It is not the same as you making the decision for them.

In more extreme situations you may feel a proposed course of action is so ill-advised that you can no longer act. That is a choice you have, but one that should only be made in exceptional circumstances.

A positive future focus

Your client wants to come away with the belief that something positive can emerge for their future.

How to provide what the client needs

Appointment letter

Before the client has come to your office, the right tone can be set by a letter confirming the date, time and place of the appointment, with a map attached showing the location of the office. The letter can be given warmth by mentioning that you look forward to meeting the person concerned and helping them with their situation.

Reception

As with so many things, first impressions can be critical. A sullen or uninterested receptionist in a forbidding waiting area will reinforce any nascent prejudices the client has about lawyers. We have all been in the office where the client is clearly an unwarranted intrusion on a busy receptionist's day. Family law clients are particularly sensitive to this because they are at a particularly sensitive time in their lives. The receptionist needs to be able to project a warm and sympathetic interest in ensuring that the client is comfortable while waiting. If there is going to be a significant wait, a cup of tea or coffee should be offered. Comfortable chairs, appropriate reading material (not just the *Financial Times* and *Business Insider*) toys, better still a play area (but be careful to identify the fact that you are not taking responsibility for children by an appropriate written notice), all signal that you are interested in providing a supportive environment.

Meeting the client

You are probably busy, may have come from an extremely difficult telephone call, but this is still this person's first meeting with the one to be told "their story". Yes, you should smile warmly and/or shake them by the hand, check they had no difficulty getting here, perhaps offer a cup of tea or coffee. Initial behaviour is important in putting across the qualities looked for, and in establishing trust.

The interview room/your office

A crowded room with files scattered on the floor and you behind an eight foot high and wide desk might make a good set for a Dickens television adaptation, but does not provide an appropriate environment. If you are in any doubt about the effect this has, try a visit to the room of a senior colleague with that colleague seated on the writer's side of the desk and you on a hard chair in front. The physical barrier to communication is obvious and the whole thing resonates with experiences of the headteacher's study/bank manager's office. It may be preferable not to sit behind a desk. The side of a desk or table is fine. The client at the top of the table and you at the side of the table is fine. The idea is not to make you feel important and in control, but to give your client the confidence to give you the information you need.

First names /surnames

There are different views about this. We appreciate that there are advantages to using first names: not least it may feel more natural and put your client at ease. Nevertheless, on balance the use of surnames, certainly to start with, tends to be advisable subject to some qualifications. The way you address someone significantly changes the way you relate to them. As a professional adviser, you should be offering sympathetic but dispassionate advice; you are not a friend but you do care. If you use first names, the boundaries, either consciously or unconsciously, can become blurred for you and your client. The client may be hurt that "Tom" is not prepared to agree with what he or she says, take up the cudgels, or at least let his or her spouse know how strongly he or she feels. The client may phone to share with "Anne", blow by blow, the details of the latest altercation but then be disappointed to receive a rather large bill for the privilege of doing so. (It is extraordinary how often the most familiar client is the one who questions the service you provide.) A client is entitled to sympathy, reassurance and concern. You are entitled to retain a professional distance. The qualities of concern and sympathy can be communicated without the use of first names and the bottom line is your client will benefit most from a sympathetic rapport with an objective adviser, acting within clear professional boundaries.

There will be exceptions. If someone uses your first name to you it may be a little contrived to insist on using a surname when your client is resolutely using your first name. However, even here, there are occasions when, no matter how informal your client, your instinct is to stick with his or her surname. You should not be afraid to follow your instincts.

The most common exception is someone who patently has an appropriate understanding and respect for your role in the situation. If you feel that communication with that person is easier and more natural on first name terms then follow your instinct if it is not going to jeopardise your objectivity.

You might say friends are another exception but our view is that under most circumstances you should not act for a friend. If you do act for a friend, you are likely to change the nature of the friendship irrevocably and not necessarily for the better. You will inevitably find it difficult to remain objective and to give advice which your friend might well not want to have. Your friendship and friend would be better served by a referral to the best family lawyer you know in town (aside from yourself!)

The meeting

Having a structure

You know the qualities your client wants and the interview is your vehicle to demonstrate them while doing your job. In order to reassure, inform, give confidence and provide a positive future focus you need information. A structure is important because it gives you and your client something to return to if the innumerable tangents available in family law cases are to be returned from. It makes sure you don't miss a vital point to be dealt with. Most importantly you provide a foundation on which an overview can be built and which you as an adviser can return to when necessary. With time, as new glosses and information accumulate, that initial overview may be extremely important for you to keep a perspective and sense of the significant points to the situation.

A client may well want to pour his or her heart out to you and you could quite happily sit there for three hours and allow that to happen. You can end up with a massive amount of irrelevant detail and without essential information. Time has to be paid for. If you explain why you are approaching things in a structured way the client will usually understand.

The use of structure does not obviate the need for acknowledgement and understanding. It is a matter of experience and practice as to how far you allow a client to follow a tangential path of significant importance to them before gently, and with acknowledgement of the importance to them of the tangential point, bringing them back to what you need to know. You have to balance the desire to let your client express him or herself with the responsibility to provide good advice and to avoid landing your client the cost of a three-hour interview.

A theme returned to time after time in this book is keeping the client informed. Keeping the client informed relates not just to what you are doing in the large-scale but also at the small-scale. It is good practice to tell your client at the start of the interview what you are going to do in the interview, how long it is likely to take, what is covered and in what order. It is essential to confirm that you will give an opportunity to discuss any additional concerns your client has not covered within the structured approach. Our experience is that people appreciate structure as long as they know what the structure is going to be and that all their concerns will be addressed.

The order of the discussion

Different approaches to the order of discussion can be equally valid.

One approach is to deal with the reasons for the breakdown in the relationship, then the children, then finances. The reasoning is that the breakdown is likely to be the most pressing thing that the client wants to talk about. It is likely to be a negative subject with strong emotions attached. The children can bring things back to a more positive focus and positive emotions with an acknowledgement of mutual concerns about residence, contact and other issues. Financial information can then be brought out with the more positive reasons for needing it having been elicited immediately before.

Another approach is to get practical information about the finances before the information about the children on the basis that with the strong negative emotions relating to the breakdown it is better to have a time gap before talking about children. The financial information may have a bearing on what you discuss about the children. Getting financial information between talking about the breakdown and talking about the children gives a space before finishing with an emphasis on what are, hopefully, common aims to do what is best for the children.

Either at the start or the end of the interview depending on your assessment of priorities for the client, you need to discuss costs.

The bottom line is you need to find an order of discussion that you are comfortable with and provides the best service to your client.

The stages of the meeting

Stage 1	Starting off and using a Questionnaire
Stage 2	Costs
Stage 3	Background to the relationship breakdown
Stage 4	Financial information
Stage 5	The children
Stage 6	Drawing things together with an Action Plan

Starting off the meeting (Stage 1)

The best way to start the interview is to ask for a brief indication of what the client is looking for advice on. This is your opportunity to gauge what sort of state your client is in, what is and is not pressing for him or her, how much time will be needed and the like. It is the first golden opportunity for acknowledgement, normalising and reassurance. Let them know that you see how difficult a time it is for them. Make a point of telling them that you are confident you can help them with their situation and find options to resolve it. Explain how you intend to structure the meeting and the stages to it.

The questionnaire

Once you have your initial information about what the problem is, it is very useful to use a *pro forma* questionnaire. Having a form to fill in means things are not overlooked. You need to note down personal details about the client, the former partner and if relevant any current partner, their children and their finances. If, after appropriate acknowledgement, you make a start with this practical information it can help the client move into a more analytical frame of mind. It is important to reassure clients:

- the information is just to let you know where they stand
- they remain in control of what if any action should be taken
- you know it is unlikely they will have the full picture; an outline is enough at this stage

Avoid giving much legal information or being diverted into taking information about the relationship at this stage.

Costs (Stage 2)

It is important that your client understands what your time costs. Most clients paying for your time privately are likely to be apprehensive. A clear explanation confirming your hourly rate, some general idea of the likely costs for the action proposed and an indication as to how costs can be kept down should be given. Although we have included this information at the start in our suggested format it may be that with some clients it makes more sense to cover the information towards the end of the meeting.

You need to make sure you have explored the availability of assistance through the legal aid scheme and explained how the system will work in their circumstances. In particular you need to give the client a broad idea of any costs they may be liable for.

It is better that your client knows about costs at the start so that he or she can make an informed decision on how to use your time. In the event of concerns arising about costs later it is better for you to be able to point out to your client that you confirmed costs the first time you met. The art is in giving the information while not appearing obsessed with money.

Background to the relationship breakdown (Stage 3)

Once basic personal and financial information is safely gathered in in a questionnaire you can move on to the next stage. The reasons for the breakdown of relationships are legion, and your responsibility at the first interview is to get as objective a picture as you can of the reasons particular to your client while ensuring that your client's emotions in the situation are properly acknowledged. The art is in the meshing of the skills of personal engagement and understanding with the information-gathering analytical skills we are more used to deploying as lawyers. Both sets of skills are equally important in facilitating a positive meeting for your client.

You need some clarity. If it is a couple who are "not getting on" you need to know precisely how that "not getting on" manifested itself. If a couple were "arguing all the time" you need to know what about, how often and what behaviour occurred. We have seen "arguing" used to cover everything from the smallest verbal fallout to significant physical violence. The amount of detail required will depend on whether the client wants to consider applying for divorce or protective orders now, in which case a fair amount may be required, or put divorce on the backburner while financial and child related issues are sorted by negotiation, in which case clarity, but not huge detail, may well suffice.

Whatever information you are getting, get it in chronological order. Ask when things started going downhill and move on in time from there. If appropriate, note specific details of significant incidents and check if there are any witnesses. Remember that clients don't know what may or may not be important in law. You must ask the relevant questions to get relevant answers. On the other hand, the client knows what is overwhelmingly important to him or her and that may not be significant in legal terms. Information which is important to the client cannot (and should not) be suppressed but it does need to be carefully managed if it does not have any legal consequences. Avoid appearing to dismiss such information. Recognise the importance to the client by saying something like:

- it must be very difficult to accept that
- it sounds very hurtful
- what a distressing situation to deal with

The type of expressions you will find yourself using will often be very general and straightforward. The choice of words has to be yours based on what you understand of your client. The delivery of the words has to be genuine. Make sure your client knows the emotions he or she is going through are not abnormal. Explain that you do need some other information to complete the picture and gently move back into information gathering.

Be careful not to belittle or negate the uniqueness of your client's experience for them. Be careful about using expressions such as "I know how you feel" or the like. You don't!

You need to be particularly careful to ensure that you are sensitive to the possibility of domestic violence. There is a relatively low level of disclosure to professional advisers of such behaviour. If there is a hint of this being an issue, you have to be prepared to clarify what has happened. There is a temptation to shy away from exploring a subject that may be embarrassing or difficult for both of you. However it has to be tackled. If information is not coming through with more general questions then you have to be prepared to ask, as sensitively as you can, direct questions. Family solicitors have to live with the nightmare of waking up on a Monday morning to read about the death of a client at the hands of their partner, having failed to obtain protective orders the previous week. You have to identify your own strategy for the particular client, but one way into exploring violence as an issue is to actually mention how often it is not disclosed and how difficult it can be to disclose it, while explaining how important it is for a professional adviser to know about it.

At the end of this stage, you should give the client a clear general outline of the law and what the general options available are for taking the matter forward. How you outline the law depends on the particular client but to do it in the simplest language you can find is never wrong.

Finances (Stage 4)

It is useful to have a checklist of all the obvious possible types of property or debts belonging to a couple. You can then run through the list checking off each type and finally ensuring there's nothing else you have missed. The fact that you have done this can avoid embarrassment, or worse, a potential negligence claim at a later stage.

It is a good idea to check what paperwork is available to support figures given and to discuss what verification might be required.

At this earliest point urgent dangers need to be spelt out. Joint bank accounts usually involve joint and several liability. Should they be closed? Contents of houses can "disappear" in a client's absence. Is there an inventory of contents? If not should one be made up?

The client needs a general outline of the law as a basis for future discussion. Again, use the simplest appropriate language you can. It is often possible even at this early stage to explore general options for sorting matters out.

The children (Stage 5)

Children are often the greatest source of anxiety and conflict on separation. On quite a number of occasions, however, clients do not want advice. Your client may tell you that arrangements for the children have all been sorted. It is tempting to leave the subject. You do need to do more. If the "sorting out" is impractical, at odds with the legal framework or the financial aspects then it is likely to become "unsorted". It is best to address potential problems before rather than after they happen.

You can usually carefully feed in appropriate information on the effects of separation and divorce on children (see Chapter 9). Your client needs to know that the steps taken over children at the earlier stages of separation can seriously affect parental relationships with, and levels of involvement in, the lives of those children in the future. Discuss what the children know and might be told. If children are to be spoken to you need to go over the best way of doing it.

The father who sorts it out by not seeing his children for several months after separation to let things "settle down" needs to know that he could well be prejudicing his chances of getting the generous level of contact with those children he envisages for the future. He should be helped to think through what the children might be making of the situation. He needs to consider the consequences for the children of his actions. Equally, the previously uninvolved father who is pressing for lots of contact, needs to weigh up the benefits and disadvantages for the children of what he proposes.

Again appropriate legal information should be given. This is your perfect opportunity to stress looking at what is best for the children. This is the time when couples can be brought to realise that they have a mutual goal in achieving what is best for the children.

Drawing things together (Stage 6)

You have obtained a full picture of your client's circumstances. At each stage you have provided appropriate legal information and advice. You have explained the cost of your time. Your client has had the opportunity to clarify any points or ask any questions he has remaining at the end of your structured approach. Your client needs to know where things go from here.

Do not promise what you cannot deliver. The solutions to family problems will almost certainly involve acceptance of lower standards of living and other elements that are not the client's ideal. Equally solutions can bring to a close an unsatisfactory and unhappy period in life and open vistas for a more positive future.

Your client wants to know his or her options and in setting out those options you need cover the major possibilities. The client may well not know what he or she wants. It is important to let the client know that that is fine. The client should be given, as appropriate, information about agencies for relationship counselling whether as an individual or as a couple, before or after separation, or with a view to reconciliation or coping with separation.

A perfectly valid option is to do nothing and the client should be supported if that is his or her choice. People often want to reflect on where things will go. The most hostile person can become conciliatory and the most conciliatory person hostile in the space of minutes, days, a week or months. It is usually helpful for the client to pause, to come to terms with change, understand the implications of that change, and decide on the best way forward. Unless there is a pressing need for contact with children to be re-established, protective measures obtained or the like no immediate action needs to be pressed on the client. The client might wish simply to think things over or may need to gather in some further information.

It is important to summarise information given and check understanding. If you are in doubt ask your client to confirm his or her understanding of matters to you.

Action points—positive future focus

Make sure that each of you knows what the other is going to do and when. If a letter is to be sent to a spouse or spouse's solicitor, is the client to see it first? Let your client write down action points for which he or she is responsible. Run through your action points. Action points give a concrete future focus.

The conclusion of the meeting needs to be positive. That does not mean promising the world, but does mean reassuring a client that he or she is in safe hands, the situation can be resolved, situations like it have been resolved in the past and you will be there to help them resolve their particular situation.

By giving a client and yourself practical tasks, by allowing a client to envisage different future options, by gathering appropriate information, by enabling them to test the feasibility of different options, you are providing new alternative pictures which may be more or less palatable but are at least preferable to the black void so often looming before he or she saw you. You are allowing the individual who came to your office anxious and depressed to leave reassured that they are setting off down a difficult, but not endless, path accompanied by a competent, caring professional.

After the meeting

Important advice to your client should be confirmed in writing. It is useful to remind your client of the broad options available for taking matters forward. It is good practice to send a terms of engagement letter including information about costs, responsibility for their case, what to expect from your firm and the like.

Conclusion

- Clients want a reassuring atmosphere from the moment they enter an office
- A structured approach to first meetings works best
- Check for understanding and action points to take things forward
- Confirm important information and advice in writing

CHAPTER 5

METHODS OF DISPUTE RESOLUTION

*"Our agenda is now exhausted. The Secretary
General is exhausted – All of you are exhausted – I
find it comforting that, beginning with our very first
day, we find ourselves in such complete unanimity."*
Paul Spaak addressing the first
General Assembly of the United Nations

Introduction

As a family lawyer you will be dealing with people who are going
through a time of transition. Many things will have to be sorted
out. There are a number of ways of doing this. The common
elements are a need for information and resolution. There has to
be some way of working out what clients need to know,
assembling the information and deciding what should happen
next.

There are some unilateral steps that can be taken. Beyond that
lies the possibility of mediation, negotiation, arbitration and
litigation. There are benefits and drawbacks in each process.
Particular factors might rule in or out certain choices.

Clients will value a realistic assessment of what is involved in
each process. The more they know about the ins and outs, the
easier it will be to see which process or combination of processes
is the most appropriate.

Some aspects may be decided by means not of the client's
choosing. It is then helpful for the client to understand the process
and the input which can be made to give them as much sense of
control as possible.

Unilateral steps

It is always helpful to consider what clients could do under their
own steam to improve a situation where a conflict or difficulty
has arisen. That may only be the first of many steps or in some
circumstances be all that is needed.

Sometimes knowledge can be a solution in itself. If someone has a mistaken belief that they lack rights, perhaps in relation to housing or children, their feeling of insecurity could make them unnecessarily vulnerable and start causing an imbalance in a relationship. Knowing their true position (without necessarily rubbing their partner's nose in it!) could restore a healthier balance. Someone who is feeling unsettled in the relationship and uncertain about the future may decide to try to work at the marriage, rather than dismantle it, if they talk through the impact the separation could have on their children or find out the financial consequences.

If a client recognises that his or her own behaviour is causing problems within the marriage, the legal consequences can be confirmed, but some information could be given about resources available to help the client tackle the problem, such as support groups or counselling.

Financial problems can cause serious difficulties in relationships. Sometimes information about benefits which could be claimed or help in dealing with creditors could take some of the pressure away.

Where physical abuse is an issue, exploring any steps which can be taken to secure physical safety is important. Alerting neighbours to call for help can be useful. A personal alarm may be reassuring. Safety can come from unexpected sources. A client who had despaired of freeing herself from a violent ex-partner was trying to lead a more peaceful life. One afternoon, her ex-partner arrived, uninvited. He did not take the trouble to ring the doorbell. He forced an entry, thundered down the hallway, using colourful language, towards the sitting-room where he could see the client. What he did not see until he burst into the room was that she was surrounded by a dozen or so other women of various ages who had been in animated conversation over the children's clothing which was the focus for a party plan being run by the client! This scene of particularly female domestic tranquillity did more to deflate the violence of the moment than a team of policemen. The reaction of mirth from the policemen who did arrive further punctured the aggression! This may not be a transportable strategy and care would have to be taken over the type of party!

Sometimes simply leaving might be the only and best practical option. If that is the case, trying to secure appropriate possessions but also to minimise the impact on the partner is an important balance. It is not only humane but also sensible to avoid anyone returning to their home and finding their partner has left and taken various items with them with no explanation whatsoever. Suggesting that your client arranges, after leaving, to have a message delivered to his or her partner by a suitable third party might be appropriate. Remember this is not a licence to clear the house—it is a way of avoiding risk of damage to personal or important possessions to be weighed against the risk to further meaningful dialogue.

Moving on from unilateral steps, parties might wish to deal with matters as informally as possible. Direct discussion at the time of separation can be very difficult. Mediation might be a more viable option.

Mediation

The process of mediation is described in more detail in Chapter 10. Mediation is sometimes called "assisted negotiation". In mediation, people who have a dispute sit down with an impartial third party to identify what has to be sorted out, gather in the necessary information, look at options, and work out mutually acceptable proposals. It is not intended to be a grudging compromise. Mediation is not a linear process of finding a mid-point. It is an energetic attempt to identify common ground and find creative solutions.

A mediator is a facilitator rather than a referee; a catalyst, not a judge. Using specific skills, the mediator enables the parties to identify how they feel, recognise how the other person feels, gather and process information and search for solutions which will meet the needs of all concerned as much as possible from available resources.

Although mediation has been around for a very long time, the more recent momentum towards family mediation originally arose in relation to child related arrangements. The importance of parents co-operating was recognised and mediation was identified as a good means of achieving better parental understanding. Mediation was seen as a way of changing and improving relationships for the future although using a task focused approach rather than a counselling one. Since then alternative dispute resolution including mediation has become more widely accepted. Mediation is used in a commercial and international setting. The problem-solving aspect has become more prominent.

Mediation is flexible enough to accommodate the potential for both improving relationships and solving problems.

In mediation, the mediator has responsibility for keeping control of the process but the outcome is the parties' responsibility. During the process, information is gathered in as a joint exercise. Each party contributes his or her part of the jigsaw to make up the whole picture. Gaps in information can be identified and plugged.

The focus is on the present and future, rather than the past. A backwards glance might be needed for appropriate ventilation of strong emotions or to clarify some information. There is no independent fact-finding or verifying of information.

The legal framework is a benchmark. Parties are encouraged to take into account both the legal provisions and their own sense of values. A lawyer mediator will provide information about the law but not advice to either party.

Once the possibilities have been explored and a formula has emerged a summary of the proposals will be prepared by the mediator. The discussions are confidential and the summary of proposals will be non-binding. Usually the couples advising lawyers prepare a binding contract based on the proposals from mediation.

Benefits of mediation

One profound benefit is a sense of well-being which can arise when people are given back control over their lives. Mediation allows people to take a full part in planning their own future. This can have a substantial spin off for children. It is reassuring for young people to see their parents being able to sort things out between them. It is a good message that adults are able to cope with loss and change otherwise young people may feel they have little chance of dealing with life's problems. If their parents are able to deal with one another as adults then the young people can go back to their role as children rather than act as go between, allies or shoulders to cry on. In turn, parents will feel a profound sense of relief if they find the impact of the separation cushioned for their children.

Another benefit is that mediation usually allows a better understanding to arise. The couple may not approve of or agree with one another but find it easier to agree to disagree and accept the other person's position. Without that, there is a risk that each will see the other in caricature and continue to try to make sense of what has happened by blaming the other person. Moving past that stage can allow the good bits of the relationship to be remembered and retained. It lays down necessary lines of communication for the future if there are any children involved.

The information gathering can be much easier when done jointly. Locating elusive financial details (and insurance policies!) often needs input from both parties. Each can help the other work out what details are required. Even if the need for full disclosure is accepted it can take a long time to assemble all the information through advising lawyers. When the fact-finding is done in parallel it allows checking and expanding of information in a non-confrontational way. Points can be clarified that might otherwise have become a source of friction. Seeing the picture emerging can start a process of reality testing leading to more realistic options being explored at the next stage rather than unrealistic positions being adopted.

Considering information together can in general avoid unnecessary friction arising. Anxieties can be identified and discussed rather than fester then erupt into an explosion of accusation in correspondence. Usually, couples have their own spheres of influence. One may have more control over and information about the children and another over the financial aspects. One may deal with homework and the other medical issues. One may look after the day-to-day expenses and the other take to do with the bigger decisions. The process of mediation can allow this shifting power to be held in balance. All areas are considered in parallel. The sharing of the information can provide powerful reassurance.

Once the information is available it is easier to look for creative solutions with the energy of both involved at the same time. If a couple look for ways that their separate futures might work they are likely to generate more workable options than if each decides what he or she would like in isolation. It is more difficult to integrate two separate plans than "fine tune" a joint one.

Mediation can avoid the misunderstandings which tend to arise from correspondence. Things said in mediation may well come across in a way that was not intended but that will normally be identified at the time by the mediator and the opportunity given to clarify and communicate better.

Where mediation is appropriate the process can help minimise the negative impact of emotions and contain the financial cost. Energy can be devoted to problem-solving rather than proving who was right!

Drawbacks of mediation

Participation in mediation does require an ability to accept the other person will have their needs taken into account and that space must be found for both points of view. Although that will normally be true of any negotiation the impact of it will tend to be cushioned where the negotiation is being carried out through third parties (except where the needs and point of view are forcefully set out in an incoming letter and a copy of that is sent out to your client!) It may be difficult for your client to accept that as an explicit starting point if he or she is still feeling very hurt and raw about the separation and still making sense of things by putting the other person only in the wrong. It is rare in marital breakdown to find a definitive answer to what went wrong and establish one truth but it can take some time to reach the stage of accepting the need to look to the future for solutions rather than to the past for answers.

Another pitfall is the need for commitment from both. Both need to agree to use mediation or it cannot get off the ground. There is no compulsory mediation. Even if a referral is made to mediation by court the only compulsory element is to attend an initial meeting, not to go through the whole process.

There is always a risk that someone will use mediation as a delaying tactic to try to gain advantage. In similar vein, mediation might be seen as a way of trying to effect a reconciliation.

A more insidious risk is of a power imbalance with the process being used by one to bully the other without the buffer of an intervening advising lawyer Although efforts are made to exclude from mediation relationships where that is likely, particularly where there has been domestic violence, power can be wielded in subtle ways. One partner can continue a pattern of control established during the marriage. Guilt may make one partner feel overwhelmed by the presence of the other. Depression might make one person withdrawn and unable to properly participate.

Problems might crop up in connection with information gathering. There could be a reluctance or refusal to provide relevant information.

The ultimate safeguard in mediation which could be an answer to some of the drawbacks is the lack of a binding outcome. Plans emerge as proposals, not contracts. That could be perceived as a weakness, particularly if the proposals are not sufficiently clear. In that case further negotiations may need to be carried out leading to costs being duplicated.

Mediation—role of advising lawyer

Beforehand

The first point is to check carefully if the mediation process will be helpful for your client. Explain what the process involves. Check if your client would be able to express their views in front of his or her partner. The test is not so much if the client would feel upset but whether he or she could express how he or she feels. Explore the pattern of decision-making when the couple were together. If your client has had very little input to decisions about any aspect of the marriage or children try to work out how to establish if it is likely to be possible to put things on a more equal footing in mediation. Was the lack of involvement imposed, a matter of choice or by default? There can be some cases where mediation is an extremely valuable vehicle for change in the pattern of communication but a degree of self confidence is necessary.

Recognise that where there has been a history of violence in the relationship it is unlikely Mediation will be appropriate. If the separation has triggered uncharacteristically heated arguments for the first time and your client still sees a chance of restoring constructive communication check that steps will be taken by the Mediator to avoid risk of confrontation on arrival and departure.

Advising lawyers have a vital complementary role. It can be very valuable for a couple using mediation to already have a broad grasp of the legal principles especially if these have been described in terms of a spectrum of possibilities. If you give a client who is going to use mediation some preliminary advice remember to mention the worst as well as the best possible outcomes. It would also help to let your client know what his or her partner's solicitor might be advising. You can start the process of information gathering particularly by encouraging your client to ask for details like pension information which could take some time to be available.

Emphasise that mediation is not about apportioning blame. Explain that the mediator's job is not to decide what happened in the past but to help the couple plan what would be best for the future.

During

There is no direct line of communication about the discussions in mediation between the advising lawyer and the mediator. Your client might want to clarify points which have arisen in mediation. The mediator might also have suggested to both parties that it would be helpful to take advice from the legal advisers. They would normally be encouraged to find what range of possibilities the law might offer. Further help may be needed with information gathering. Arrangements might have to be made to obtain a valuation of a business. Your client may well wish to talk through proposals emerging from the mediation process. Once you have considered the prose and cons you could help formulate questions to be raised in mediation if any aspects of the embryonic proposals seem unclear.

After

You will normally receive a written summary of proposals for resolution of the issues and perhaps a summary of financial information prepared by the mediator from your client at the end of the mediation process. You can check if the outcome ties in with the stated aims. If the proposals seem wide of the legal framework see if there is an explanation for that in the summary. If not, check the position with your client. You will be preparing the formal Agreement and taking responsibility for the legal content of the document. It is very important to double check that the outcome is acceptable and appropriate. If there is something you cannot understand and the client cannot clarify or if some of the proposals lack detail you could suggest that you client arranges a further mediation appointment.

Negotiation

Life is an almost continuous process of negotiation. All parents are only too acutely aware of that. For most people the day will often start with an energetic unilateral negotiation about when to get up! Whenever there appears to be competition for available resources the need for negotiation will arise. Negotiation in family law is usually taken to mean tackling the issues which have to be sorted out after a separation with the use of a professional intermediary who explains and discusses the legal framework with his or her clients and promotes their interests in attempting to secure an agreed outcome. Information will have to be gathered in and possibilities explored. For most family lawyers a significant part of the work will be dealing with negotiations. It is a very flexible method of dispute resolution. There are no set methods but certain styles can be identified.

Negotiation styles

- horse trading (I know you want the house so you can have that if I keep the policy and my pension)
- Dutch auction (I want the house, the policy and to keep my pension)
- war (whatever you want, you are not getting it)
- win/win (let's look at ways we can sort out arrangements for the house, the policy and my pension that make sense for all of us)

Win/win (or principled) negotiation sits very well within the family law framework which has fairness as the benchmark and where in many cases there will be a continuing relationship between the parties after the negotiations are over. It involves looking for solutions which will accommodate the interests of both parties which in many cases will be complementary rather than in conflict even although that may not be immediately obvious to your client.

Methods

Negotiation usually involves a mixture of correspondence, telephone calls, more frantic communication by fax and more informal exchanges by e-mail together with meetings with your client and sometimes varying combinations of participants. Once information has been gathered in it can be very useful to assemble both parties and the two solicitors under the same roof. It is usually best to avoid starting off with everyone in the same room. If the solicitors have some general discussions followed by individual meetings with the clients involved and matters are developing positively a round table discussion could allow emerging proposals to be "fine tuned". If everyone is in the room together from the beginning tensions are liable to rise and your understanding of the client's instructions at any point may be hard to rely on unless telepathy is your strong point.

Negotiation is a demanding and rewarding skill. Some basic strategies can be learned. There is nothing to beat experience.

Benefits of negotiation

One great benefit is that negotiation allows you as advising solicitor to act as a buffer (being an emotional punch bag is not part of the job description!) You can try to neutralise the impact of correspondence which you know is likely to press the wrong buttons for your client. You can absorb the general anxieties by providing specific information which will often reassure. You can filter out the more unrealistic extremes of attitude and expectations diplomatically.

Negotiation fosters co-operation. It encourages problem-solving and gives clients emotional space to adjust. Clients can be supported with information and advice. They have access to the legal framework and remain in control of the outcome and, to an extent, the pace.

Drawbacks of negotiation

If negotiation is not carried out in good faith by all parties then its strengths can become its weaknesses. The negotiations can be prolonged indefinitely and create continuing anxiety and mounting expense leading to no specific outcome. Time and cost can become a nightmare.

Disclosure of information can be like drawing teeth. Details may not be made available or only partial disclosure made. Clients may feel so worn down by the delay that they consider agreeing settlements without the information (probably as planned and to their detriment)

It can allow the legal framework to be body swerved. The fact that a particular proposal may be light years from a client's entitlement can be met in negotiation (as it cannot in litigation) by "so what—that's my best offer".

Correspondence may be—wittingly or unwittingly—abusive. Some letters written contain florid language which would grace of Victorian melodrama but certainly do not entertain a modern client (or his or her solicitor)

Inexperienced or opinionated solicitors may constipate progress by giving either too little or too much direction to their clients

Bullying can be carried out by either inappropriate threats in correspondence or in conversation with the client direct creating an atmosphere of fear rather than problem-solving.

Arbitration

Arbitration involves the appointment of a person of the parties' choice to decide on a dispute between them. It is a method of dispute resolution which probably pre-dated the formal court system and is based on contract.

Parties may include a clause in a Separation Agreement referring any dispute or difference which may arise to an arbiter. Such a clause usually nominates an office bearer of an organisation like the President or Vice President for the time being of the Law Society or the holder of a specific judicial office to select and appoint an arbiter at the point a dispute should arise. It would also be open to parties to select an arbiter to deal with any dispute which has arisen.

There is no set wording for a reference to arbitration. The Law Society of Scotland operates an arbitration service and provides styles of arbitration clause, submission and agreement.

Once a submission to arbitration is made the arbiter has a very wide discretion on the procedure, within reason. It can vary from being dealt with by written submission alone if the parties agree through written and oral submissions to a full heating with witnesses.

Benefits of arbitration

Arbitration could allow the selection of an individual with specific knowledge and experience to decide a dispute. It can allow flexibility and speed where the court process might be cumbersome and drawn out. An enforceable decision can be made promptly and privately.

Drawbacks of arbitration

The arbiter appointed has a high degree of control over procedure. The parties can no longer have control over the outcome they had in negotiation nor be quite clear what the framework will be in arbitration. It can become delayed and can be expensive. The arbiter's time has to be paid for as well as the legal advisers and any witnesses.

The role of legal adviser in arbitration

The first thing is to help the client decide if it will be appropriate to include an arbitration clause in any agreement.

The next step, if an arbitration clause is triggered, is to advise about a choice of arbiter if that is left to the parties. Knowledge of the law for the particular issue, a good analytic mind and a brisk approach to life are all useful qualities in an arbiter!

The preparation of the submission to arbitration is the key task. The background and issues to be resolved should be set out with precision and clarity re-read from the point of view of someone who has no prior knowledge. Does it still make sense? If not—back to the drawing board. A perceived benefit of arbitration is speed and efficiency but that will be helped by a clear joint submission. From that point keep on top of any information requested and keep within given time limits.

Litigation

Where there is a high level of conflict, a significant dispute over fact or a complete impasse with negotiation it is likely to be necessary to seek a court's decision. Litigation presents a very structured means of resolving disputes. There is a significant degree of formality. The process involves fact-finding and the application of a set of rules to those facts. Although there may be an emphasis on disclosure of information, to a degree each party is expected to assemble whatever information he or she believes important.

Benefits of litigation

If your client has good cause to feel children or assets may be removed against his or her wishes a protective court order will provide reassurance. Where factual matters are very relevant and two utterly contrasting versions are failing to gel into any coherent picture independent adjudication may be necessary to make any progress. If delay in negotiations is being used tactically or the gap in the spectrum of possibilities is proving too wide to bridge it can be better to seek a decision in court than allow the drain of an unresolved dispute to continue indefinitely.

The strength of a court order may be the only means to obtain protection against physical harm. It may be needed to ensure an enforceable outcome.

Where one partner in a relationship has tended to dominate and take decisions for the family the other partner may need the buffer of both of advising lawyer and the court process to feel confident of obtaining full disclosure and a fair disposal.

Drawbacks of litigation

Although the court process will provide a structure, the timetable may be rather elastic and delays are quite possible. Procedure will be set down but there will be elements of discretion and decisions might be made about the procedural aspects that are none too welcome for your client.

Costs tend to rise once parties enter into litigation and the possibility of being found liable for the overall costs becomes a risk.

The disposal is entirely outwith your client's control. The outcome might please only one or indeed neither party!

Litigation is necessarily an adversarial process. Claims and allegations will tend to inhabit the more florid end of the spectrum of possibilities. This does nothing to improve co-operative parenting or allow a couple to have some good memories of their past even although they having no future together

Litigation—role of advising lawyer

The advising lawyer in litigation takes on a very demanding role. You should seek to state your case assertively but without aggression. You must cope with the formality of court procedure without allowing matters to become impenetrable to your client. You need to pursue your aims vigorously but remain objective throughout. Although the "people skills" which are so very necessary in other areas of your practice as a family lawyer are also vital here they must be put to use in a more probing and fact-finding way. You have to be steeped in the substantive law and be thoroughly familiar with the procedural rules.

Appropriate dispute resolution

So how is the client to decide which is the appropriate method of dispute resolution? To a large extent the strengths and weaknesses of each method tend to deliver the answer to that question:

- If there is a reasonable degree of co-operation mediation or negotiation are likely to be appropriate. Mediation is particularly appropriate where children are involved.
- If it is clear that your client is still very hurt and angry or was never involved in decision-making during the relationship or would find it hard to express their views, negotiation would probably be more appropriate.
- If there is the history of domestic violence negotiation or litigation are likely to be appropriate.
- If there is clear indication of a lack of frankness from your client's partner or risk that assets might be used or moved litigation may be necessary.

The crucial thing is to help your client choose the right way forward for him or her in the particular circumstances. In most cases there will first be an attempt to resolve matters using mediation for reasonably articulate and self confident clients or negotiation for those clients who prefer or need more support because of their own or their partner's temperament, with litigation as the alternative should that first approach fail to provide a resolution.

Remember that the objective is the resolution of disputes, not fuelling disagreements, and finding solutions which will stand the test of time.

CHAPTER 6

CREATING CHOICE

"It isn't that they can't see the solution. It is that they can't see the problem."

G.K. Chesterton,
The Scandal of Father Brown, 1935

The early stages

Introduction

This is where the inner game of family law is played out to the full. Although there are usually a number of options in any situation of change, choice is very much a state of mind rather than an exact science. Clients may start off feeling that they can see absolutely no way forward. Part of your job as adviser is to enable them to see that there are in fact a range of choices. The next step is to prevent your client starting a search for the Holy Grail of one right answer. There is an element of helping clients like what they get rather than getting what they like.

It is important in the early stages of advising a client to create a climate of problem solving rather than fire fighting. If a client can start seeing the possibilities and not just the difficulties then negotiations will be easier and more constructive. There is more energy in being proactive than reactive.

In this Chapter we look at the process from the client's perspective. In the following Chapter we re-examine the process from the solicitor's point of view.

Generating initial options

There is a process in generating options. Although much of the process will unfold naturally, it is worth standing back and analysing the component parts. It should then be easier to work out what is wrong if a client seems unwilling or unable to look at possibilities which you can see emerging. There are more on analysis in the next chapter but taking a broad approach the normal sequence is:

- doing the groundwork, including acknowledging and normalising
- gathering in factual information
- providing legal information
- identifying needs
- exploring possibilities

Only at that stage should detailed options start being identified. Any earlier and people will make premature decisions based on either emotion or incomplete information. In either case it can be difficult for them to start looking at other plans which may be more appropriate in the long term. It is fine to accept possibilities as they arise as long as they are labelled "provisional". Leave room for manoeuvre.

When working towards generating options it is important to keep an eye on:

- timing
- cost
- client's values

When you start looking at detailed possibilities make full use of lateral thinking and brain-storming. Humour and metaphors can aid creativity (see Chapter 7). Draw on your legal knowledge and other background resources.

Groundwork

Part of doing the groundwork is clarifying your role as legal adviser. It may seem at times like equal measures of parent, psychologist and lawyer! An important point is that you are not there as your client's friend. You are there as adviser. A friend has been defined as someone who knows all about you and still likes you. Your job is to help clients understand themselves and the law. It is not to work out whether or not you like them. Nor is it to unquestioningly sprint off in the first direction the client indicates he or she wants to go.

It can be helpful from the outset to make it clear that you can offer the client useful information, help with looking at possibilities and guidance about the consequences of different choices. You will not tell them what to do—you advise rather than instruct. You will help them get back into the driving seat. Most people feel out of control when things go wrong in relationships. It can be very helpful to reassure clients that they can get back in charge. It is important to make it clear you will give them support in doing this with information and guidance. Initially people may feel very overwhelmed with what has happened. Their starting point could be to look for someone to wave a magic wand. Most clients will value help in picking up the reins of their own lives again. You may find a client who continues to resist taking that step and who seems unable to absorb or process information. He or she might want to hand over all responsibility. In those cases it is sensible to diplomatically:

- check what support network of friends and relatives they have
- ensure they are aware of counselling and support organisations
- if seriously concerned about how they are coping, find out if they are receiving medical help
- encourage them to make full use of those resources

There may be the odd occasion when after you have gone through the preliminary stages with a client you recognise your approach will simply not suit. It is better to acknowledge that sooner than later. Where that happens a client will usually accept the position and arrange more compatible representation.

From the beginning you have been careful to acknowledge the client's feelings without endorsing their interpretation of events. Remember to maintain that position. Although it is important to assess the impact of a partner's behaviour on the situation it does not help if you start making criticism of the partner (or his or her legal adviser!) from a personal point of view.

Make it clear to clients that they are allowed to change their minds. Sometimes clients feel they are letting you down if initially they want one thing and later decide on another course. You may have to say quite frequently that you are there to help them work out the possibilities and to use the legal framework to achieve whatever outcome seems most workable for them, not you!

Although the choice of outcome (within the range of possibilities) is the client's responsibility that does not let you off the hook so far as the process of getting there is concerned. It can be much harder work to help a client arrive at an informed choice than to simply tell them what to do. And you can always let them know which of the options seems to you to deliver most of what the client appears to want, with the caveat that you realise you are assessing it from outside while they will have to live with it from the inside

Factual information

Full information gathering is a very important part of this process. Possibilities or restrictions may be overlooked otherwise. Asking the right questions is as important as giving the right answers. Clients need to be told what further details they need to clarify. It is also crucial to have a way of keeping your client information up-to-date and accessible.

Legal information

As well as recognising the need to explain the law in a way that is relevant and understandable, family lawyers are faced with the daunting task of ensuring that their knowledge is kept up-to-date. It is always good to be able to provide an immediate answer. It is essential to provide the correct answer! Far better to tell a client you need to do some research than say something you later have to change or modify.

The legal framework does tend to provide a spectrum of possibility rather than any one answer. Explanations to clients should make it clear when you are explaining the legal rules and when you are outlining your own interpretation of how they might apply. It is usually necessary to preface your assessment of how the law might affect a specific client by emphasising that the interpretation is based on your experience and knowledge. It is informed but not infallible!

It can be helpful to add what your client's partner might be told about his or her legal position. Doing that will prepare your client to hear their partner outlined a very different version of the law. It will also prevent you from taking too over-optimistic a reading yourself.

A client will expect you to know what the law is now and of any definite or possible changes in the foreseeable future. There may be developments in other areas of law that could have impact. Speed-reading is a useful attribute!

Remember that in the same way your client will be provided with an action replay of their partner's visit to the lawyer so will your comments and explanations be broadcast extensively throughout a network of friends and relations. Clarity and moderation in your approach can help the impact be informative rather than explosive.

Identifying needs and confronting fears

At this stage, and in negotiations, it is very important to focus on interests rather than positions. Encourage exploration of what your clients realistically need rather than reinforce what they believe initially they must have. The earlier you "reframe" a client's wants into legitimate needs the better. In most cases the fear of losing a particular house or a specific amount of income or a current level of involvement with children can be seen and identified as a need for suitable housing, a reasonable standard of living and a continuing importance as parent. Preferences about how that may be achieved can be acknowledged and opportunities taken to flag up that there could be other ways.

If you can encourage a client to be flexible in approach the process of negotiation will be easier and more rewarding. To be flexible demands a level of self-confidence and composure. Those are qualities which rarely co-exist with fear or panic. This underlines the importance of the preliminary stages of acknowledgement and reassurance followed by reframing and encouraging the client to paint a picture of the future rather than replay the video of the past.

It is also necessary to distinguish needs from wants or demands. Reassurance does not mean false guarantees. Usually clients' fears conjure up Doomsday scenarios. They fear the worst. It is enough to negate that without promising the best. Stick to bread and butter predictions. Let jam be a bonus!

On the other hand, some clients may express expectations far beyond anything the facts or law could deliver. When you are at the stage of explaining the reality of the situation go round to work. Break the news gently but honestly. The client may actually realise and expect the truth.

Exploring possibilities

The final stage before considering options in detail is to check that there is enough information available about any broad possibilities which have emerged. This is still at the level of generalisation: the price of houses in an area, not identifying a

specific property to buy, the kind of money a client could raise
rather than an offer of loan.

It is quite a difficult balance to strike. Once clients start
investigating specific possibilities there is a risk that events will
start developing the life of their own. An irresistible house will
present itself on the market; a particularly good mortgage package
will materialise.

The problem of insufficient information is delay and
frustration.

This highlights the importance of appropriate timing.

Timing

Time is a factor throughout the solicitor-client relationship. A
client will want to know how long things will take. Although it is
obviously impossible to give a precise estimate you should be
able to say how long different stages usually take. It is important
to emphasise how dependent this is on factors out with your
control. Bear in mind that if you were to ask a builder to quote for
an extension you would ask the cost and timescale. You would
recognise that factors such as the weather were unpredictable, but
still expect a reasonably reliable indication of how long the work
would take.

Equally, be careful not to force the pace. Clients are usually
adjusting to significant emotional and practical changes. They
may need a breathing space at some point. Watch for any
indication that a client feels things are going too fast. It may
be necessary to mention benefits of having things sorted out
sooner than later. Always emphasise that is a tactical
consideration and must be balanced by the client's actual
experience. Point out long and short-term advantages and
disadvantages in delay.

Cost

Clients will most certainly want to have some idea of costs.
Although it is very difficult to be accurate with any estimates it is
entirely reasonable for the client to need at least a broad idea.
They will have to be provided with information about the basis of
your fee charging. Realistic estimates with timely reviews if
circumstances change are very important.

Clients' values

What is important to the client may be different from the legal priorities. A client may value co-operation over capital, peace more than property. Some particular items may mean much more than their monetary value. Not being dependent may be more attractive than receiving financial support.

The crucial test is the client's underlying motive. It is one thing to relinquish potential claims as a positive choice yielding a sense of benefit albeit non-material. It is quite another to give up rights out of fear or fatigue.

If clients seem motivated by escape from a bad situation check they do know of alternative strategies that would not involve giving up claims. Ask them to imagine how they might feel looking back in two or three years' time. See how they might feel if a subsequent partner were to obtain the benefits they will be losing. Make sure this checking does not seem like bullying. Emphasise you just want to help them make sure they are making the right choice from their point of view, not yours.

Guilt can be another factor inhibiting a genuine consideration of possible options. If that means decisions are made that are later regretted it could poison parental relationships in the future. Again, asking clients to consider how they might feel about their decision looking back can be a useful test.

Remember that your role is not judge but adviser.

Lateral thinking

Law tends to be very linear. Sometimes thinking sideways can be more fruitful! On occasion, solutions can be found well away from the legal landscape. As a starting point it is important to encourage people to bear in mind:

- considering other avenues
- taking a different slant on things
- presenting their partner with options

Considering other avenues

Sometimes there is an opportunity for input at a very early stage. The client may be quite clear that things are not right at home, but totally unclear what might help. Family lawyers are a vital gateway to various other agencies. Information about individual and couple counselling may be as helpful as information about legal rights although it is important to give both. If parents are having conflict over how to deal with teenage children there are organisations able to help with guidance and support. Tensions can arise in step families and again, help and support can be given. At an early stage, it can be very important a client who is either not working or working below their capacity to start making serious inquiries about career prospects. Sometimes a separation may seem inevitable but particularly daunting if a client has been very much based at home. Building a social network and acquiring some practical skills could be an important first task. Keep a list of local organisations and be prepared to widen your area of exploration.

Taking a different slant on things

Helping clients see things from a different angle can open a whole new range of options for them. They may believe that any issues to be resolved must create a winner and a loser. Introducing the idea of and/and rather than either/or can lower the temperature and create space for problem solving rather than fire fighting (see Chapter 7). Point out that there are usually options which allow a reasonable outcome for everyone. Their partner may choose to see it in a more confrontational way. The client need not accept that reading. The client cannot control their partner's attitude but can control the impact it has on them. Agreeing to disagree may be the most effective strategy!

Presenting their partner with options

One choice is to let the other person choose! Giving a partner the option of counselling or separation, the possibility of mediation rather than litigation or negotiation rather than court proceedings can avoid impasse. The client must be willing to give their best shot to whichever choice is made.

Any alternative strategies should always be in addition, not instead of, legal information.

Brainstorming

Another technique to open up possibilities. Particularly if the options seem rather limited suggest to the client that you bounce ideas off one another. Make it clear that you should both just say anything even if it seems quite unlikely. Have ten minutes or so of coming up with proposals good, bad or indifferent without stopping to evaluate. Only at the end have a look at what has emerged. Some of the wackier ideas might be quite unworkable as they stand but prompt thoughts of more sustainable possibilities. It is important to insist on no editorial control at that initial stage!

If things were very stuck asking for fantasy ideas might result in the chance of a modified version of the fantasy turning out to be quite workable.

To take it a little further you could suggest a quick burst of considering what options the partner might suggest if present. Looking at things from the other person's point of view can yield up positive as well as negative results. It also builds in some reality testing. The same exercise could be carried out in respect of any children that are affected. Probably a more sober stage.

In the end there should be a number of ideas. Various elements are likely to coalesce into something approaching a few real possibilities. They will almost certainly need further thought and investigation but it is a significant step in the right direction. It should also help lighten the atmosphere. Brainstorming tends to be quite fun which can be a benefit in itself.

Humour

Being able to see the funny side of a difficult situation can be the best therapy available. Expecting a client to be able to do that before they are ready could severely test the solicitor/client relationship! As always with humour, timing is the key factor. Using humour against yourself can be a useful role model but even that, if used too early could dent your credibility. It is always better to find ways of seeing the absurdity of a situation rather than belittling the other person.

Healthy humour can shrink fears and release energy. If it becomes malicious the whole approach to problem solving can be restricted by a lapse back into defining people as goodies and baddies. It can be a short-term gain with long-term disadvantages.

Another risk is of inadvertently causing of offence. Test the water carefully and be very ready to apologise at any sign of outrage.

The leaven of humour can be a boon. Equally, humour can be a dangerous element in an unstable situation. The main thing is to be true to your natural style with a filter of caution.

Metaphors

Law tends to be a very wordy business. The use of metaphors can be another very helpful leaven. A dissertation on dividing matrimonial assets risks being rather indigestible. Talking about sharing out the matrimonial cake can be easier to swallow. A lighter touch also makes humour easier. You can both consider the risk of leaving only crumbs if the division is clumsy.

Clients may feel swamped by the amount of information in circulation. If you talk about the exercise being like fitting pieces of a jigsaw together it can give a sense of purpose.

Metaphors can be useful in acknowledging and testing the emotional climate. You can comment that a situation may create the feeling of being under a pile of sand or wading through treacle. If the client nods emphatically you will have helped by recognising their feeling of helplessness. It will also alert you to the need for a sense of progress.

Metaphors can allow probing and bring comfort. It is helpful to build up a good stock.

Reality testing

Let the facts do the work. Reap the benefit of careful information giving and gathering by allowing the realities of the situation impose a shape on the possibilities. Fears of poverty which seem overwhelming in abstract are likely to diminish when figures are worked out. Utter resistance to moving out of the matrimonial home may shift when arithmetic discloses alternative accommodation could allow a better standard of living. Child care plans can be revealed as unrealistic by asking gentle but probing practical questions rather than by launching an attack (which would almost inevitably spark a robust defence!)

Face saving

No one likes being wrong. Initial reactions based on emotion and lack of information can make people ricochet off in an unhelpful direction. Try to help clients leave themselves enough space to change direction without feeling that they're backing off.

It can be useful to emphasise how much separation is a process rather than an event and that as people find out more, what made sense to them initially quite often changes. Explore things in a way that allows the client to see for her or himself that their attitude could be destructive in the long run. The object is not to prove that you, the legal adviser, are right and the client wrong. The real aim is to allow the client to find the right way.

Clients are likely to start off feeling that to make sense of the situation he or she must show their partner is in the wrong. There may be an assumption only one of them can be in the right with an enormous investment in being that one. You can carefully acknowledge the frustration and difficulty of the situation and ask if it might be more workable to accept that each of them at this point may have a different understanding of what has happened. Explore the possibility that it might be better for the client to use available energy on working out a plan for the future rather than trying to seek for truth in the past. Widen out the spotlight of blame into a more general illumination of possibilities.

Other solicitors don't like being wrong either! If some initial correspondence reveals an obvious misunderstanding of fact or law feed in the correct information as diplomatically as possible.

Conclusion

Once you have done the initial ground work with your interview skills and exchange of information, helping clients see the possible rather than impossible in a situation is the next stage in problem-solving. It is a vital step towards more formal negotiations. Remember to:

- Focus on interests, not positions
- Encourage flexibility and exploration
- Help save face!

CHAPTER 7

ANALYTICAL SKILLS

"Many people would sooner die than think. In fact they do."

Bertrand Russell

Creating choice for clients requires solicitors to be conscious of the underlying dynamics of our work.

Every minute of every day in our own particular way we take in information, process it and reach decisions. It is something we do so often and do so naturally that it may seem perverse to suggest that we should do it differently or could do it much better. Having said that, a cursory examination of human history and current human behaviour suggests that, whatever the processes gone through, the wrong decisions are often made. Family law decisions are no exception. In dealing with our clients we cannot ensure that the right decisions are always made. We can try and ensure that the processes and skills employed leading up to those decisions are the best available to minimise the number of wrong decisions.

Identifying the analytical components, the skills and processes underpinning your work is useful, in that if you know what skills and processes you use, you can explain what you are doing to your client. If you are not making progress, it may allow you to see which one of the components is failing and identify how it can be used more effectively.

The building blocks of analysis

The starting point for the process of analysis might be an identification of the materials needed:

- the law
- the facts of the particular situation
- the motivations of the client

Family solicitors know the law or can find it out. We clarify the facts of the situation as we go along. Some of the personal motivations we encounter could be grouped something along the lines of:

Emotions/feelings

Anger, hostility, jealousy, sadness, contentment, anxiety, bitterness, loneliness, love, concern, satisfaction.

Thoughts

"I am worthless." "I am useless." "I cannot survive on my own." "I hate confrontation." "I hate uncertainty." "I am strong." "I am in control." "I am satisfied." "I am dissatisfied."

Practical needs

"I need money." "How will I get appropriate housing?" "What will work for the children?"; "How will I feed the family?" "How will I support myself?"

All these elements have their own force and need to be given an appropriate place in the analytical process.

Emotions

By identifying both positive and negative emotions you can see how they influence choice for your client. Negative emotions are the most common. The client who is filled with anger towards the adulterous husband may be determined to get a divorce based on that adultery. That is their choice. Your job is to explain the advantages and disadvantages of pursuing that particular course.

By recognising negative emotions you can help your client move on from some of the more negative ruts they have fallen into. Most importantly, if there are serious emotional problems and/or a desire to seek appropriate help in coping with the fallout from family problems you can refer the client to the right place for that help.

Just as importantly positive emotions can be used to move a client on. They can provide the motor for acceptance of available solutions. The husband who feels intense anger against the wife who left him can still accept options that may benefit his wife indirectly but also give a practical expression to his love of his children.

The fact of the matter is in all our work we move in and out of the undemarcated realm of emotion. We cannot ignore it, we have to acknowledge it as part of our analysis and realise that legal solutions can only provide a part of the overall acceptance of divorce/separation for a client.

Thoughts

It is difficult to draw a clear boundary between the emotional and psychological. The Shorter Oxford English Dictionary definitions talk of the emotional as connected with "feelings or passions" with the psychological as "pertaining to the mind". Thoughts can in theory be separated from emotion, but are nearly always accompanied by, or are the result of, some sort of emotional excitement, and vice versa. The battered wife may well feel anxious and lacking in self-confidence. She may think she cannot survive on her own away from the battering husband. It is a combination of emotion and thought. How many of us have seen battered wives return to the battering husband precisely because of a lack of self-confidence which, perversely, has been brought about by the very person she has been made too afraid to leave? We can acknowledge the thought and the feelings that come with it while trying to point to possible solutions.

If a female client comes to see you, rendered almost unable to act because of her lack of confidence, you can offer up your experience to both identify the problem and reassure on the possibility of a solution:

> "Many people have been in your situation over the years and violent behaviour does knock down a person's self-esteem and make them anxious. The thing is it can become a vicious circle. Because your partner is violent you become anxious, because you are anxious and think you cannot cope, you stay with him and because you stay the behaviour continues. I can help you out of that sort of circle but the decision to use that help has to be yours. No one can force you to act. What I can tell you is that many people who have chosen to confront the situation have realised quite quickly that they can cope, they can move on, and they can be content again. The most difficult part is often the first step."

You are offering an appropriately limited (limited to what is appropriate for a solicitor) insight into what psychologically can happen to people in the situation. You are making it clear that the decision as to what to do is the clients. You are also saying that other people have been in the situation and have pulled through.

By making it a generalised, rather than specific, assertion you are not taking responsibility for this persons robustness or offering a view on their personality (a view that you are not professionally equipped to give).

The practical

This is the area where our primary energy has to go and where we can have the most positive effect. However in dealing with it what we come up with will reflect the weight we have given to other less tangible areas of concern. It means identifying priorities for childcare, housing, money (short-term and long-term), and other practical concerns, weighing their relative importance and seeing how they can be met.

Law, facts and motivations

Whether we acknowledge it consciously or not in assisting our clients we are trying to help them achieve a legal outcome that satisfies practical, psychological and emotional needs in the best way possible. How far we go in teasing out and examining the particular elements or the motivations behind those needs is a matter of experience and training. The trick is to realise you are doing it without straying beyond the appropriate goal of a sensitive handling of the client into psychobabble or worse.

How the analytical progression works

Many solicitors have an instinctive grasp of how the process of resolution actually works. In broad terms, it tends to be a series of circular progressions (see Diagram A).

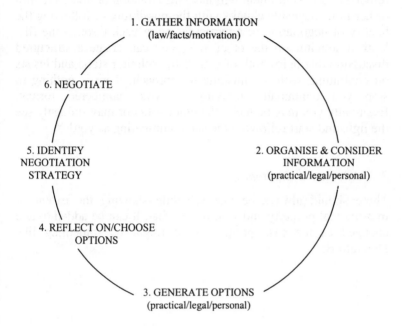

Diagram A

THE CYCLE OF PROGRESS

1. GATHER INFORMATION
(law/facts/motivation)

6. NEGOTIATE

5. IDENTIFY
NEGOTIATION
STRATEGY

2. ORGANISE & CONSIDER
INFORMATION
(practical/legal/personal)

4. REFLECT ON/CHOOSE
OPTIONS

3. GENERATE OPTIONS
(practical/legal/personal)

We will look at each stage in turn.

1. Gather information

We have dealt with this subject in Chapters 2–4.

2. Organise and consider the information

How you choose to lay out your correspondence and the information once you get it can either be a help or a hindrance. It seems so elementary as not to be worth mentioning and yet much legal correspondence proceeds on the basis of a mishmash presentation of information confusing to the solicitor never mind the client.

Using headed/numbered points

The larger the number of issues, the longer the period of correspondence, the more issues can become confused and factors be lost. If you start with numbered points and return to them remorselessly, your client will have his situation presented to him or her in manageable chunks with the possibility of following the history of negotiation or a particular point back through the file. With a solicitor on the other side, you can create a structured discussion that helps both of you. If the solicitor starts and insists on continuing with the mishmash approach, there is nothing to stop you continually replying in your numbered format. Eventually you may be lucky the other solicitor may suddenly see the light and start following the same numbering as you!

Schedules are a vital tool

There should always be one schedule showing the extent of matrimonial property and who owns what. It can be added to and changed as the case progresses. It might be something like Diagram B:

Diagram B

DRAFT SCHEDULE OF MATRIMONIAL PROPERTY

FOR PAUL JOHNSTON AND AMANDA JOHNSTON
(AS ESTABLISHED TO 14/9/00)

Date of Marriage: 10.4.80
Date of Separation: 3.11.99

ASSET	OWNER	HOW VOUCHED	VALUE
15 Pedlar Way	(J)	Graham & Hall Valuation dated 5.12.00	£200,000
Bank of Scotland Current A/C No004411840	(PJ)	Bank Statement of Account Dated 14.3.00	£ 1,500
House Contents	(J)	No vouching required	Minimal
Standard Life Endowment Policy No538491	(AJ)	Standard Life letter dated 5.3.00	£ 3,500
Pension No. 138941	(AJ)	Standard Life letter dated 15.4.00	£150,000
LIABILITIES			
Halifax Loan 2411308	(J)	Halifax letter dated 3.1.00	£55,000
First Direct Loan 320410	(PJ)	First Direct Loan document dated 3.7.98	£ 5,000

A final schedule can show in tabular form the settlement proposal
(Diagram C):

Diagram C

PROPOSED DIVISION OF MATRIMONIAL PROPERTY
BETWEEN PETER JOHNSTON AND AMANDA JOHNSTON

Date of Marriage: 10.4.80
Relevant Date: 3.11.99

ASSET	P JOHNSTON	A JOHNSTON
15 Pedlar Way		£200,000
Bank of Scotland		
Current Account 0044		
11840	£1,500	
Standard Life		
Endowment No 5384941		£3,500
Pension No. 13841	£150,000	
Total:	**£151,500**	**£203,500**

Liabilities		
Halifax Loan 21411308		£55,000
First Direct Loan	£5,000	
NET ASSETS HELD	£156,000	£148,000
Payment from PR to AR	£4,000	£4,000
	£152,500	**£152,500**

Flow charts

These can show ownership of companies, history of contact arrangements and the like in an easily digestible form (Diagram D):

Diagram D

HISTORY OF CARE ARRANGEMENTS FOR SOPHIE AND JAMES THOMSON

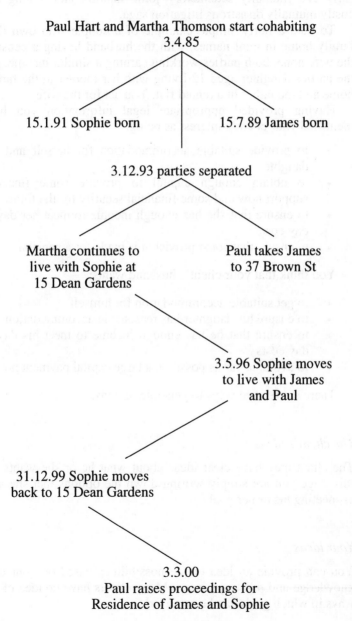

Paul Hart and Martha Thomson start cohabiting
3.4.85

15.1.91 Sophie born   15.7.89 James born

3.12.93 parties separated

Martha continues to   Paul takes James
live with Sophie at   to 37 Brown St
15 Dean Gardens

3.5.96 Sophie moves
to live with James
and Paul

31.12.99 Sophie moves
back to 15 Dean Gardens

3.3.00
Paul raises proceedings for
Residence of James and Sophie

3. Generate options

The ability to help a client generate options to resolve issues is of tremendous importance. It can make the difference between an early and mutually satisfactory joint solution and a long and costly mutually disastrous litigation saga.

To take a fairly simple example of a couple who own their family home in joint names, with the husband having a pension, the wife none, both parties working earning a similar income, and the parties daughter aged 12 living with her mother in the family home and the father in a rented flat. You act for the wife.

Having provided appropriate legal information you have identified your client's interest as being:

- to provide suitable accommodation for herself and her daughter
- to obtain enough capital to provide some financial support now and some financial security for the future
- to ensure that she has enough income to meet her day to day costs
- to ensure that some provision is made for a pension

You think that your client's husband wants:

- to get suitable accommodation for himself
- to ensure his daughter has reasonable accommodation
- to ensure that he has enough income to meet his day to day costs
- to avoid, as far as possible, a large capital payment now

There are several ways to generate options.

The client's ideas

The client may have clear ideas about what he or she wants. At this stage you are simply writing down the options that she sees as meeting his or her goals.

Your ideas

You can provide an idea of the possibilities based on your own knowledge and past experience. Many clients have no idea of the ways in which goals can be achieved.

Brainstorming

We can be so constrained by our normal way of thinking that options can be overlooked. The licence given by brainstorming to offer up any idea, however apparently absurd, can lead to surprisingly good solutions. It can't be done in a half- hearted way. The imagination has to be given full licence in an atmosphere without judgement.

The available options and variations on those options will probably emerge quite quickly. For your client in the example given they might be:

- buy the family home and provide a capital payment for it now
- sell the family home and use the capital to buy another appropriate property
- stay in the family home with some mechanism for giving capital to the husband at a later stage

Having generated these basic options, the offshoot from the cycle of progress (see Diagram A) would be more information gathering about new issues that have arisen such as the attitude of the mortgage-holder to a potential transfer; the availability and cost of alternative accommodation; the availability of other mortgage facilitates; the possibility of finding other sources of funds. Information would also be needed on what income would be needed to meet day-to-day costs under each option (projected income and expenditure) and how the income could be attained. Finally a realistic assessment would have to.be made of whether any capital could be obtained as well as how any pension provision could be made. Having obtained the relevant information, you are in a position to move on to the next stage.

4. Reflect on/and select options

At the stage of selection it is particularly important to reflect on all elements of your client's interests. One way to make things clear is to actually draw up a "cost /benefit chart" (Diagram E):

Diagram E

COSTS/BENEFITS OF PARTICULAR OPTIONS
FOR MRS CORMACK

Option 1	FOR	AGAINST
Buy the house and provide a capital payment now	• Stability for daughter • No need to move • Good investment • Clean break	• Expenditure re mortgage (affordable?) • Too big for long term • Need guarantor? • Bad memories in house • Difficult getting capital for husband
Option 2 Stay in house and give capital to husband at later stage	• As above • Avoid need to go find capital now	• As above • No clean break • Need to pay husband later
Option 3 Sell the house and use capital to buy another property	• Clean break from past • Less expenditure on mortgage • No guarantor • Capital issues resolved now	• Change for daughter • Change for client • Change in schools for daughter

If not a chart, then a résumé in writing to your client setting the costs and benefits out clearly is useful for him or her and a helpful reference point for you.

5. Identify negotiation strategy

There are many different ways to identify a strategy for negotiation. It is helpful to know three things:

The client's ideal option: what your client would like to happen at best in the knowledge of the relevant legal framework.

The client's realistic outcome: what your client can realistically expect in terms of the law and the circumstances particular to them.

The client's fallback alternative: what your client would agree to at worst, rather than have the matter decided judicially (this element will often shift as a final court hearing draws nearer!)

6. Negotiate

We discuss approaches to negotiation in Chapter 8.

Other tools

Images

It may be difficult to get your point across or to show how you have analysed a situation. Simple images used consistently can help.

The pyramid

This is a useful image for discussing what for instance, an expert can do. You want to explain the benefits of a stepped approach. Looking at a business your first step might be to ask an accountant to give a broad view of value based on recent accounts. You are at the top of the pyramid and can get a costing of that step. Having looked at your first response you can decide to go down to the next level for a look at further specified information again with a costing of that step. A whole series of progressions down to the bottom of the pyramid where you are looking behind the accounts at the date used to make them up can be identified. If you have provided your client with the pyramid as an "analysis image" right at the start it will be easier for them to understand how the process works and how each level leads logically to the next level. Your client can then decide how far down the pyramid they are prepared to go.

The negotiation spectrum

If you consistently present your client with a linear image of how a situation might be resolved in Court, you are helping them to adjust their own thinking from win/lose to a range of possible outcomes with varying advantages and disadvantages. The latter is the truer reflection of reality. With information about potential costs the client can decide how far along the spectrum he or she is prepared to go in order to settle the action.

For example, if your view is that the client will attain something in the range of 40–60 per cent of the available matrimonial property and the property is worth £180,000 you can identify ideal realistic and fallback positions on the spectrum (see Diagram F):

Diagram F

THE NEGOTIATION SPECTRUM

Fallback	Realistic	Ideal
72,000		108,000
Worst possible Outcome		Best Possible Outcome

Total Value £180,000
40% = 72,000
60% = 108,000

The spectrum line does not need to be drawn for the client. They can easily retain the image in their mind. Compare this with the win/lose approach and it is easy to see the terror and entrenched positions that can result.

A father looking to resolve a contact dispute presented with a win/lose view of his situation might have some of the thoughts set out in Diagram G:

Diagram G

WIN	LOSE
She will pay my costs	I will pay my costs and hers
I will gain revenge	I will never live it down
I will see my son at the times I want to	I might never see my son again

Your choice of image can thus help or hinder the negotiation process by opening up possibilities on a spectrum or closing things down to a yes or no, win or lose.

The calendar

Most of us will have spent an inordinate amount of time trying to sort out arguments about contact arrangements for children. It is difficult to visualise what particular arrangements would mean for each party. With the increase in the number of people working shifts the possible permutations for contact are frequently complex. In generating options for resolution it can be difficult to see how a compromise might be achieved or extra days contact given or taken. In all these situations a calendar can be helpful. You can, for instance, sit down with a client and circle possible extra days for contact in one colour, and days already agreed in another colour. The calendar can give you a physical image of a distribution of contact proposed.

The Pot

Many family law cases get bogged down in arguments over each individual item of property. Solicitors work item by item. They start with the house, perhaps move into pensions and then on to savings and so on. This methodology is almost guaranteed to create a series of small conflicts. If you describe and work on the process of division as involving putting all the property into a pot and then deciding which items are to be taken out for which party and on what basis with reciprocal compromises and deals on both sides you can foster the idea that the whole process of resolution involves a series of heavily inter connected trade-offs. Negotiations can progress in a more integrated way allowing a proper play between the different elements.

To take a basic example, if looked at in isolation a husband may well not want to transfer the family home to his wife. If he is getting to keep more of his pension in exchange the deal might seem more attractive. By using the "pot" approach innumerable creative solutions can be found which are not possible looking at things item by item.

Conclusion

This chapter is a brief and basic introduction into the kind of issues and processes that can be used for family clients. What we suggest may well not be the answer for you. What is required is some reflection on and clarity about the processes and skills you choose to use and how well they work in providing solutions for your clients.

- Be aware of all the elements that go into decisions for family clients
- Be aware of the processes through which work is organised and taken forward
- Be creative in how you organise and layout information
- Be creative in generating options to resolve disputes
- Use positive images to present information and decisions
- Encourage the idea of a spectrum of possible outcomes rather than a win/lose scenario

CHAPTER 8

NEGOTIATION SKILLS

"Let us never negotiate out of fear. But let us never fear to negotiate."

John F. Kennedy
Inaugural Address, January 20, 1961
(*Vital Speeches*, February 1961)

In the past much of life was spent accepting and inhabiting pre-ordained roles. Sons followed fathers in careers. Daughters followed mothers in home-making. Society was hierarchical. Now, life is a perpetual dance of negotiations within families and in the workplace. We are constantly bargaining for resources, material and emotional. Negotiation skills have become a key feature in successfully navigating modern society. Nowhere is this more apparent than in family law where clients have either chosen or are forced to reinvent themselves and their environment and are anxious to salvage as much as possible in their family and economic structures.

There are two fundamentally different approaches to negotiation. One is to see the situation in terms of winners and losers. The other is to work from a problem solving angle to create a win/win outcome where both parties achieve a satisfactory solution. The first way assumes that resources are limited, the second that a flexible approach will tend to expand possibilities.

There are some situations where there will be winners and losers. If there has been a pattern of violence or dishonesty it may well be necessary to seek remedies for your client which will not go down well with his or her partner. That will normally be in the context of litigation. In most cases both parties will have some legal rights to pursue. Any agreed settlement will normally have to include some benefit to each. Initially your clients might find it almost impossible to accept that aspect. If you use your people skills to the full they should become ready for a negotiated settlement and see the need for some joint incentive.

The win/win approach of principled negotiation was developed at the Harvard Negotiation Project. It is outlined in *Getting to Yes*, by Roger Fisher and William Ury. They explain:

"It suggests that you look for mutual gains whenever possible and that where your interests conflict, you should insist that the result be based on some fair standards independent of the will of either side" (Introduction).

A win/win approach is well suited to family law negotiations for a number of reasons:

- it reflects the broad legal approach of fairness
- it helps clients move on and stop defining themselves as combatants in a fight or as victims
- it allows the most constructive use of resources

Negotiation should be a creative search rather than a bad tempered contest.

In computer experiments it was found that reciprocal co-operation was the most effective overall strategy in negotiation. The reciprocal element is important. All giving on one side and taking on the other is not appropriate! Further concessions have to be withheld if earlier ones have not been returned. It is important to pace the concessions to ensure a rhythm of balanced concession is taking place. It makes sense to concentrate concessions on the negotiation process initially (for example the provision of information) to establish a basis for co-operation then concentrate on making concessions which will be of value to the other party and less important to your own client. Concessions which are of more significance for your own client should be made cautiously but creatively. This pattern of give and take should be a dynamic process of solution seeking, not a series of grudging compromises.

Children

The win/win approach to financial and property issues fosters a climate which makes it easier for couples to be co-operative separated parents. The focus in this chapter is on negotiation for financial and property issues. These will obviously have a bearing on the welfare of any children involved. It is always an important and sometimes delicate balance to strike between recognising the needs of children and avoiding children being used as levers. The Solicitors Family Law Association in England underline that point by setting out that arrangements for children and money should be dealt with in separate letters. Chapter 9 looks at dealing with the consequences of separation for children.

The process of negotiation

Remember that the process of negotiation starts as soon as you meet your client. By using your listening skills constructively, by the helpful provision of appropriate information and by guidance in creating choice for your client, you have already encouraged a healthy environment for negotiation. The process continues in the flavour of your initial overture or response to the other side. Your skilful communication will have provided a shining example of how language can be used as a bridge rather than a battering ram.

Negotiations are fluid but usually go through the stages of

- prior preparation
- initiation of negotiations
- information exchange
- exploration of possibilities
- adjustment of options
- setting down solutions

although after the initiation of negotiation the next three stages are usually repeated before a solution emerges. Negotiation is not a linear march—more of a circle dance!

Throughout it is important to remember that in negotiation persuasion is more effective than coercion. Keep in mind the fable about the contest between the wind and the sun. Each claimed to be the stronger. They agreed to test this out by seeing which of them could remove the coat of a man who happened to be walking by. The wind blew and blew with all his might. The man wrapped his coat closer and closer to him. It was the sun's turn. As the rays warmed him the man loosed his coat. The sun continued to beam down. The man took his coat off! Let the warmth of courtesy and civility and the energy of problem solving inform your negotiations.

Preparation

Preparation is essential to achieve successful outcomes for clients. You need to have a grasp of what factual information is available and what more is needed. Your client needs to have a grasp of the broad range of possibilities and the legal principles involved. Both of you need to have the right state of mind to make the most of the process. Find out what your client's objectives and concerns are. Avoid buying into his or her starting position about how those should be accommodated. If you concentrate on their underlying interests alternative and equally acceptable solutions are likely to emerge which may be more attainable.

It's better to negotiate towards acceptable housing which will allow children to remain at the same school than to pin your professional credibility on delivering the family home to your client. In fact, setting out reasonable objectives and exploring how they could be met, may stimulate the very outcomes sought where a bald demand would meet with unrelenting resistance. Talk through the potential best and worst outcomes whether by negotiation or litigation. Be realistic about both ends of the spectrum, particularly the worst. Clients are unlikely to be upset with you if they end up with more than they expected but very likely to be disenchanted with a miscalculation the other way!

Always check and discuss what alternatives there are if matters cannot be sorted out by negotiation. It is infinitely easier to negotiate if your client is able to accept the possibility of alternative ways of dealing with the situation if the negotiation fails. Being able to walk away or litigate if necessary is a powerful factor in negotiation. Either way you and your client need to be clear what is the best that can be done if negotiation fails. Remember to use that as a measure to check the benefit of any eventual settlement proposals.

Consider what the objectives and concerns of your client's partner might be. It may be upsetting for your client to do this. Be thoughtful and diplomatic. Speculate what might have to be taken into account if matters had to be sorted out in court after all. Invite your client to suggest outcomes a court might consider for their partner.

Keep checking that your client's objectives and concerns remain the same and if there has been a change review the options and check if any further information is needed.

Initiation

When considering what initial approach should be made the first step is to work out the state of play between the couple. Although every situation is different there are three broad categories which help determine your approach to starting negotiations. Find out which applies to your client by asking whose decision it was to separate.

Joint decision

Do not take this at face value. Ask your client what answer his or her partner would give to the same question. Quite often you will find the answer makes it clear that the partner is less enthusiastic about the separation than your client. It is fairly unusual for both parties to be at the same stage. One will often have started disengaging from the relationship quite a long time before the separation. If they are definitely both at the same stage of adjustment then it's likely both will want a co-operative problem-solving approach from the outset.

Your client's decision

If the decision to separate is wholly or mainly your client's then the entry point to negotiations needs more careful handling. Try to avoid a "shopping list" by way of first overture. Even if your client's proposals are eminently reasonable, a "lawyer's letter" itself is likely to be utterly unwelcome and its contents tainted with assumptions of conflict. Make the overture simple and emphasise a willingness to co-operate. Invite contact from the other advising solicitors with their proposals about the best way forward.

The other partner's decision

Your client may in this case want the first letter to serve the dual purpose of setting out precisely how much in the wrong the partner is and also just how much it is going to cost to atone for his or her wrong doing! It is crucial to spend a lot of time acknowledging and reframing to get to the point where your client will recognise the risk in doing that. Once your client accepts the long-term self-interest from the benefits of co-operative negotiation and is able to get a grasp of the legal framework you should be able to make a relatively neutral overture rather than unleash a judgemental diatribe. It is very important for hurt clients to be helped to understand that judgemental diatribes invariably lead to vigorous rebuttal rather than generous terms of settlement. It is also vital to avoid either dismissing or encouraging their sense of outrage. Your people skills must be put to good use at this stage.

Information

The more information which can be assembled before specific proposals are explored the better. A purposeful phase of exchanging factual information can create a useful neutral climate. Clarifying the broad objectives of the partner will help establish your credentials for joint problem-solving and let you check out if your hypothesis about the other partners interests is correct. Once the factual information is assembled the shape of a workable solution often starts emerging.

This stage can be used to check that there is a willingness to approach matters on a reciprocal basis. Reticence about provision of necessary information should stimulate caution. If you suspect bad faith at this point you can make it clear that negotiation cannot proceed unless there is a two way traffic with information.

Exploration

The initial stages of negotiations (and sometimes the entire negotiation) will tend to be undertaken by an exchange of letters or e-mails. It is usually necessary to let your clients see a copy of incoming correspondence. Most clients expect this and it's usually easier to take instructions by letting your client see the letter. "Lawyer's letters" can be powerfully destructive weapons. Keep reminding your client that negotiations can only succeed if both parties reach agreement. Correspondence should foster problem solving, not point scoring. If letters come in which your client find upsetting and inaccurate try to use that to allow your client to see how little such correspondence encourages co-operation. Recognise that some different readings of the situation may be inevitable. Correct factual inaccuracies with tact. Be firm but courteous in your replies. Bear in mind the issues outlined in Chapter 6, "Creating choice", and always look for creative ways of expanding possibilities. Encourage an exploration of suggested options rather than an exchange of mutually exclusive demands.

When making proposals don't wildly overstate but leave some room for manoeuvre. Remember to keep the thread of reciprocal co-operation. Explain how the proposals would accommodate your client's partner's needs but emphasise the reciprocal nature by setting out your client's conditions first. Link your proposals to the facts but avoid the risk of "over selling". If receiving proposals, appreciate that it is rare for anyone to put their best offer first!

Adjustment

This stage will be easier and more constructive if you have fostered a problem solving climate; your client will be more able to see possibilities in the situation rather than the prospect of a grudging compromise. Recognise what concessions your client is quite willing to make which would be important to his or her partner. Help your client recognise that give and take is necessary to achieve an agreed outcome. Sometimes bringing in other expert advice or a range of issues from pension splitting to welfare benefits will help expand the possibilities for both parties. Sometimes you may realise your proposals and concessions are disappearing into a black hole. In that case—don't make any more until you get some positive response. Keep a watchful eye on the balance of give and take. Sometimes you may recognise progress where the client with a more subjective yardstick, sees none. In that case more sympathetic acknowledging, reframing and mutualising could be necessary. Try to keep the focus on a constructive and expansive exploration of possibilities.

Solutions

When solutions start emerging make sure the detail is carefully thought through. Work out consequences and timing very carefully. Remember that your clients need workable and enforceable arrangements which will be clear and avoid anxiety in the future. If you are responsible for putting a settlement into writing always read it through as if you were acting for the other partner. Read it through again actively looking for ambiguity or imprecision. Ask your client to read it through very carefully and to tell you if there's anything that is not what they expected. Unless clients are officially given permission (indeed encouragement) to question wording in a formal document, they are likely to assume any gap between the wording and their expectations is just an inevitable part of the process.

Dilemmas

Take it or leave it

If your suggestions are being rejected out of hand, and contrary proposals are made which seem entirely out of kilter, try repeating your reading of the factual and legal situation and ask for clarification about the basis for the different view.

If this fails to stimulate a movement towards a mutual understanding double check your reading of the situation to make sure you have not gone off at a tangent (or been unable to resist client expectation).

If it still seems like a totally one-sided negotiation discuss the alternatives to a negotiated settlement with your client in more detail. If litigation could be a viable option and the client is willing to follow the course if necessary start a countdown by explaining to the other solicitors that court proceedings may have to be initiated unless satisfactory proposals can be identified within a specific time. Follow that up with a tighter timescale and the promise of litigation then make that promise come true if necessary. Never threaten what you do not plan to deliver.

It can be useful to go down that road reasonably early on if the negotiation seems to have absolutely no momentum. It can take a pending court action to force the reality of the factual and legal situation back into the picture and will often stimulate some gratifyingly energetic negotiations once the action is raised. Remember that only applies to quite extreme cases.

Embarrassment of choice

In many cases the problem will be not so much intransigence as an embarrassment of possibilities at both ends of the spectrum. If you can see the force of arguments for both parties consider if there might be other factors which could impose some shape and allow available resources to dictate an outcome.

Move from the general to the particular. Work out exactly what the gap is between the parties. See if there could be a fresh approach to achieving your client's objectives which would meet the stated objectives of his or her partner.

Try a four way meeting, assembling the clients and solicitors under the same roof with enough space to allow solicitors to confer, take instructions and re-confer with the possibility of moving towards a round table meeting. It is usually advisable to avoid starting off round the table. Discussions will tend to be awkward, tensions palpable and proposals often reneged on afterwards.

Input from an expert might be another useful way forward.

Unquantified offers

If proposals are forthcoming but information about financial resources less so it can be quite a dilemma. Your client might be nervous about losing an offer by demanding information. It is a gamble but it is to relatively rare for anyone to offer more than they think they need to do. Anyone generous enough to do that is likely to be willing to part with information. There may be ways of trying to test the water. If information is missing about pension valuation an actuary might be able to provide an estimate. If it is about income your client (or you) may have some idea from other sources. In the end the client has to make a choice based on your explanation of the pros and cons. It would be wise to set them out in writing.

Strategies

Resist bullies

Remember to stop making concessions if none are being made in return otherwise it's not a negotiation at all!

Watch your language

Avoid using "but" if possible. The word carries with it an unspoken message that the reader or listener will not like what comes next. It is usually possible to put points across using "and" instead of "but"—"we recognise your client is keen to sell the house and are aware your client believes it important to avoid a move before the children's exams". The word "but" suggests there must be an either/or decision to be made. Using "and" opens the possibility of meeting the needs of both parties.

Negotiate, don't pontificate!

If you decide to act as megaphone for your client's complaints about the situation don't expect a negotiated outcome.

Keep alert for "nibblers"!

Sometimes negotiators leave some of their hoped-for terms as a coda to the main negotiation. Points are raised immediately after main settlement terms have been arrived at. There is a real risk of concessions through exhaustion if relatively minor issues are raised at that point. Stay alert!

Distributive bargaining

There will be points in many negotiations where the exchange seems to have narrowed to haggling over some specified item or amount. Try to avoid this where possible. Aim to keep a more complex interplay of factors to be pieced together. Look out for other elements to bring in to widen it out. Think about whether timing or interest or the possibility of future reviews might open it up a bit.

Principled negotiation can work unilaterally

Don't be daunted if you find yourself up against a combative opponent. If you stick to the steps outlined and use your client's interests and legal position as the benchmarks then you can keep your side of the negotiation principled by maintaining courtesy and competence. If that fails to achieve a result you can take your competence into court proceedings.

Conclusion

- Look for the win/win outcome
- Remember your "people" skills
- Test things from the other person's perspective

Further reading

Fisher & Ury, *Getting to Yes* (Hutchinson)
ISBN 0-09-164071-7

Ury, *Getting Past No* (Business Books Ltd)
ISBN 071-2650865

CHAPTER 9

CHILDREN

"If you bungle raising your children I don't think
whatever else you do well matters very much."
Jacqueline Kennedy Onassis
Theodore C-Solenson, "Kennedy"

Introduction

Most parents do want the best for their children. Despite that,
many parents handle separations in a way that will make the
situation significantly more distressing for their children. The
main reason for this apparent contradiction is a combination of a
lack of knowledge and an understandable failure to recognise that
children and adults have different ways of making sense of a
separation in the short and long-term. Solicitors dealing with
families are involved for a finite period of time and with a limited
remit based principally on legal knowledge—adding appropriate
people skills, a broad pragmatic awareness of significant research
findings and distilled pragmatic experience can make that
involvement constructive and rewarding. Various elements can be
identified:

Information

Since solicitors are likely to be a point of contact for parents
going through separation it is very important for family lawyers
to be aware of the general messages from research and of sources
of further information and support which could be of help to
parents and young people.

Perspective

A crucial step in advising parents as clients is helping them to
disentangle their own interpretation of the situation from how
their offspring may be viewing matters. In some circumstances
emotions may be running so high as to make that task one for
formal counselling rather than advice but in many cases a nudge

in the right direction will make a radical difference to the final destination.

If you can focus on the children's needs for now and the future and do so at the right time your client may start seeing things from a very different perspective. That can have a helpful impact on both the child related issues and the wider picture.

Mediation

Since decisions about children will need to be made, not just during your period of involvement, but for many years to come it is worth trying to help the parents establish better channels of communication for the future. Mediation can be a particularly good way of doing that. Clients should always be informed about the possibility of mediation.

New partners

One common source of conflict following a separation is the involvement of new partners. Dealing with the introduction of the new partner for both the children and the former partner is a real challenge. Tackling that successfully can minimise anguish and friction for the children and wear and tear on the advising solicitor.

Legal framework

This does, in the main, embody a helpful and constructive approach. Explaining the legal rules sympathetically can be a very useful way of changing the basis of discussing arrangements for children.

Children's roles

Children can unwittingly contribute to the conflict and exaggerate the gap in the way their parents see things. You have the potential to flag that up and dispel unnecessary disagreement.

Children as individuals

Just as adults can become caricatures so can children become cyphers and lose their individuality. As part of the information gathering which is necessary you can incidentally help restore personality to the children involved by appropriate questions.

The reason it is important to ask questions about individual children is because their personality, age and stage will all be factors in helping you identify the options for possible care arrangements.

Reality testing

When clients are considering plans for their children it is important to check they are being realistic and truly thinking through the nuts and bolts of any arrangements.

Problem areas

It is useful to develop strategies for particular problems that tend to crop up regularly in relation to children. An element of lateral thinking can often be helpful. In addition to the issue of new partners two other particularly troubling areas are where children are apparently refusing to go for contact or there are allegations of abuse.

Some interest in and grasp of how families interact is all part of the information you need to be able to make sense of the picture yourself and provide advice that in turn will make sense to your client.

Recognising the suffering of children and feeling helpless to relieve their distress can be the most stressful aspect for separating parents and advising lawyers. For both categories it is important to aim for a workable outcome rather than some fairytale ending. A workable outcome can have a magic of its own.

Messages from research

A list of relevant publications in connection with the research which has been carried out into the impact of separation on children is provided. The information should be used with caution. An advising solicitor is not a psychologist. Research findings can appear to support inconsistent conclusions. There are few absolutes.

Despite these caveats, there is some useful information which can be abstracted to bear in mind as an advising solicitor.

The way a separation is handled has an enormous impact on how children cope with having their parents in separate households. The worst outcomes for children seem likely to arise from conflict and poverty as a consequence of separation more than the separation itself. Conflict between adults is particularly bad for children when the children are the focus of the conflict. Very few children would choose for their parents to separate. Parents who argue before a separation may assume their children will be relieved if they separate. In fact, children may have assumed arguments were relatively normal between parents and be surprised and dismayed when they part. That does not mean parents should automatically stay together. If they cannot have a relationship which is a good example of an adult relationship for their children remaining together may not be of ultimate benefit. It will be a double loss for their children if they separate because of arguments in general only to start focusing the arguments on the children.

Adults in general and parents in particular are very powerful figures for children. It is frightening for children if an adult who has been part of their life appears to vanish with no clear explanation. Children may then worry in case the other parent also disappears. As a result they can become very clingy. Children assume that parents know best and don't make mistakes. It can be very unsettling for children if their parents seem out of control, frightened and uncertain about the future. It is very reassuring for them if their mum and dad can still make joint decisions about them after a separation.

Children will normally love both parents and seek the approval of each. It will cause them great distress to be forced to choose between their parents.

Different ages and stages

Children of different ages and stages of maturity will react in different ways to their parents separating. Since young children believe that adults don't make mistakes they will tend to assume that anything going wrong is their own fault. The children are likely to think they are to blame for the separation. If the parent who leaves does not keep in touch their child will tend to think the lack of contact is because of some failing on the child's part. Older children may be very judgmental in a rather narrow way.

They may be liable to turn against a parent they perceive as behaving badly. Teenagers might feel frustrated about the adult problems and prone to "opting out". There are also gender differences which have a varying impact at different ages.

It is quite normal for children to regress for a while after a separation. They may start bed-wetting or being inattentive at school or behaving disruptively. They are having to cope with loss and change and it is understandable if that affects their behaviour. It is certainly not necessarily a signal that contact is not working.

Repeated changes

These become increasingly difficult for children to cope with. The more change, the more a child is stretched and may reach breaking point if the changes are too frequent and significant. If the parent the child lives with has a sequence of failed relationships it will be difficult for that child to maintain self-esteem and equilibrium.

Violence

Relationships where there has been significant violence can lead to particularly troubled outcomes for children. Children who witness domestic violence are liable to be damaged by the experience. Contact following a separation can in some cases be used to continue an abusive relationship.

Continuity

In most cases children will benefit from continuity. Contact which is conducted with a modicum of courtesy and co-operation will reassure children of their parents' continuing ability to manage things on their behalf. If parents are able to explain a separation to children in a way that does not make out one or both parents to be bad and also avoids the children feeling responsible; if they emphasise the continuing love both parents feel; if they make manageable arrangements taking their children's views into account, then separation need not be a blight for their children.

Disentangling views

The first step is to help your clients recognise that each of the adults and children involved will have a different reaction to a separation. In general it is best to acknowledge what a big change has taken place and how everyone must be working out how to adjust to it. Recognise that your client will be keen to help the children deal with the separation as well as possible. Say you have some general information which might be of help to them when they are deciding how to tackle things that crop up. Let them know that children can give some misleading messages in the aftermath of a separation making it more difficult for parents to get things right. Usually clients are eager for guidance and will encourage you to say more. It is much easier to go into a dialogue about children which has been invited by the client in this way rather than imposed. The client is much more likely to be receptive to the information. Try to avoid appearing to criticise your client's interpretation. It should be possible to accept their reading of the situation as one in good faith and allow for the possibility that by exploring other information and explanations their interpretation will change.

Adult perspective

Sometimes it may appear as if one of the parents and their children are all in the same boat. The client may describe herself or himself and the children as having been abandoned by the other parent. He or she may exhibit a "siege mentality", describing how well the household is getting on without the other parent. You may be told that the children never mention the other parent.

Children's perspective

Recognise aloud how much the children must love the client and be upset about what the other parent has done. Mention that it would be hurtful for them to think that they don't matter to the other parent. Gently explore the possibility that the other parent may love the children in their own way even if their behaviour seems to contradict that. Speculate that it could be helpful in the long run for the children to overcome the hurt of what has happened at this stage rather than store up their anger. Then point out tactfully that, although the client has the possibility of a new relationship, the client's former partner will always be the children's natural parent. The children could have a wonderful relationship with a new partner but they will still have to make sense of where their natural parent fits in. Most parents do understand the benefit of avoiding children feeling bitterly ashamed of, or angry at, one parent.

You could also mention that children tend to worry a lot about their parents and will probably be feeling very protective towards your client. Say the children will want your client to be all right and be happy again. Tell your client that it might be very helpful if he or she can reassure the children that although things are difficult they will get better and plans will be made to get things on an even keel.

Non resident parent

If you are dealing with the parent who has left the house, that parent may play down the impact of the separation on the children and see any difficulties arising as the result of the other parent's bitterness. Explore the possibility that the children might be finding the separation a big change which is difficult to deal with. They might not want to upset your client by expressing hurt or upset if they are now only spending a short time with him or her. If your client has been important in the past (which will normally be accepted) it would be likely their children might feel a sense of loss. Mention that they might talk about their upset to the parent they are living with.

No parenting pattern

A particularly difficult situation is where parents, often very young, have not lived together after the birth of their child. The young mother may feel very dismissive of the young father's competence. The young father may feel very angry and excluded. The extended family may be mirroring and distorting these views.

In discussing matters with the mother it is necessary to explore the nature of the difficulties they had as a couple. If the relationship was a violent one and any interactions since the birth of the child marked by abuse towards the mother, there are questions over whether contact is appropriate and the level of risk involved. Suggesting arrangements which would ensure your client and the father need not meet could help test the intention of the father and make it less likely that contact would be pursued simply to control the mother. In view of the age of the child it would necessarily involve another adult familiar to the baby and an environment where that adult felt secure, possibly a contact centre. The logistics may militate against such an arrangement.

If the father is young and inexperienced with children, it may be necessary to encourage the client to consider the potential benefit for the future in helping the young father improve his parenting skills rather than discouraging him and being reproached for that in later years by the child. Explore what might happen if the child did search out the father later on. By then, the father might seem entirely acceptable and the child could feel cheated of the opportunity of having had a relationship during the intervening years.

When advising a father in this situation it is necessary for him to recognise the importance of co-operation rather than confrontation. It is good to acknowledge the benefit of his involvement in the longer term while underlining that in the shorter term the main help he could give is to support the mother. Emphasise the need to build up a relationship with a baby over a period of time and point out the benefit to him of the mother seeing him in a positive light during that period. Talk through the practicalities of the care of a young child in some detail. A heated pursuit of "parental rights" can become a more measured attempt to be a parent when the discussion starts focusing on nappies and feeding times!

Mediation might provide a setting where parents could develop more confidence in one another.

Resident parent

It is not uncommon for the parent with care, in most cases the mother, to resent the lack of involvement the other parent is showing. She may feel that she has been left with the responsibility of running the household and disciplining the children. The father may appear to her to be having all the benefit and advantages of the life of a single man, spending money on social activities and fitting the children in as and when this suits him rather than considering the children's needs. You may be very well aware that when advising fathers in similar circumstances, the account you hear is that the mother has been left with everything including the house and children, is receiving a sizeable chunk of their income by way of support, yet still makes difficulties over the meagre contact they now have with their children. It can be helpful when advising either parent in this situation to share this insight with him or her. Explain that sometimes you advise mothers and sometimes fathers. Say what a different interpretation each tends to make. Speculate that the parent left with the care of the children will naturally be very aware of the work and responsibility while the one who is not in the household will be acutely aware of their lack of involvement.

Many of the difficulties which arise from contact arrangements are a result of each parent looking through a different end of the telescope like this. Neither parent is entirely in the right, neither is entirely in the wrong. Much energy can be spent focusing on the differences. From the children's point of view the energy would be much better used in searching out the common ground. Mediation can be a particularly good way of doing this.

Mediation

Encouraging parents to sit down with an impartial mediator can greatly increase the likelihood of emotional and practical resources being used for the benefit of all concerned rather than dissipated in bad tempered dispute. If you have helped a client to start seeing things through the eyes of their children mediation will be all the more productive. It is important to have up to date information about local mediators.

Conflict

If there are serious concerns about whether contact could be workable because of the degree of conflict or uncertainty over the other parent's competence through inexperience as a parent, it is important for those issues to be on the agenda. The discussion should not immediately focus on what contact there should be. If the client with care reports an impression that the mediation appeared to start with a discussion about when rather than whether contact should take place it is worth encouraging your client to take that further at the next mediation session. Although the mediator may have tried to facilitate discussion about the concerns raised by your client it could be that your client found it difficult to articulate the anxieties but did not come across as lacking in confidence. Mediators will always try to ensure a balance in mediation but there can be cases where some imbalance is not detected. If you explain that to the client and ask if they felt they could try again to put their point across it may still be workable to use mediation. If a client feels unable to make their point at mediation than it is unlikely mediation should continue.

Obstacles

In many cases mediation will be about what may seem to outsiders to be "fine tuning" but may involve issues which are presenting apparently insurmountable obstacles to mutually acceptable arrangements. The process of mediation is likely to allow these obstacles to diminish to a workable degree. Far more detailed arrangements can be made using mediation than normally emerge from a traditional negotiation. Children's lives can be very complex. They may have a range of out of school and social activities. There may be various medical aspects to be taken into account. Asthma and its attendant paraphernalia of inhalers and such like merit quite detailed discussion.

One of the more challenging aspects of using mediation to discuss children is that the sense of loss and hurt felt by the children tends to come into sharp focus. That can be very painful for the parents. Most parents genuinely wish to prevent their children coming to harm. It is difficult for them to accept that their own behaviour has caused grief. Once they do face up to that it is possible to start making plans which will allow the children's sense of loss to diminish and for them to regain a feeling of being loved and well cared for. Parental denial is not the route for children to navigate separation successfully.

Another aspect which can be successfully tackled in mediation is dealing with the extended family and circle of friends.

Extended family

Grandparents, aunts, uncles and cousins can be very important for children. One of the sad things about separation is how easy it is for one side of a family to disappear from the lives of children. There is a tendency, which is understandable but potentially very destructive, for friends and relatives to show their support for one partner by criticising the other. Insults are traded and become indelibly marked on the minds of all concerned. It is not uncommon to find that the client has moved on and wishes to enter a more co-operative relationship with their former partner but is having difficulty in doing that because their family and friends see it as a betrayal of their earlier support.

Advising lawyers can help prevent that situation arising. Your impartial acknowledgement of the client's distress and problem-solving approach can demonstrate a way of helping which does not require a punitive appraisal of the partner's behaviour. So long as your initial interview is with the client alone, it will allow him or her the opportunity of expressing their hurt and upset and hearing it acknowledged rather than reinforced. It allows the client the chance to explore the mixed and apparently contradictory feelings which will no doubt be around for them. It enables a client to make a start planning for the future rather than dwelling on the past. If a client is accompanied to the office by a close friend or relative, although excluding the friend or relative from the main interview, you can offer the opportunity of summarising your discussion in their presence at the end. In doing that you involve the other person and at the same time provide an example of how support can be given in a way that focuses on future possibilities rather than past hurts and can be different from simply taking sides.

This does not mean glossing over bad behaviour. Recognising that a parent has taken steps which are destructive or said things which are hurtful may well be necessary. Setting boundaries of acceptable behaviour in terms of courtesy and reliability may also be necessary. The significant difference is trying to minimise the impact of that behaviour for the future rather than to maximise the degree of blame which is likely to keep all the energy focused on the past.

If you take statements from friends or relatives you can take the opportunity of acknowledging the benefit of their support and tactfully reinforcing the more impartial aspects of that. Sometimes the taking of the precognition itself will help put a more neutral slant on things. You will be focusing on the factual elements and on occasion doing this will remind the witness of the previous importance of the other parent to children. It might highlight how much the difficulties sprang from the adult rather than parent relationship.

Anything you can do to help your client's wider circle adapt at the same pace as your client will yield benefits in the arrangements which have to be made about the children. It is one thing to have contact times set down in writing; it is quite another to achieve arrangements that work. If your knowledge of the legal framework leads you to give advice which is undermined by friends and relatives, your relationship with the client may become strained and the file beset with a flurry of telephone messages and communications by fax or e-mail urgently signalling problems with contact visits.

If, after all this, matters still have to be resolved in court, the climate should be less angry and more factual. It will allow witnesses to provide information which has more impact because it is less freighted with accusation.

New partners

Resident parent

The introduction of a new partner to children can be a legal and emotional minefield. Where the parent who has the children living with him or her acquires a new partner, the other parent may feel enormously threatened both as an ex-partner and as a parent. It may be the final signal that the adult relationship is over. That alone may be devastating. In addition, it may seem as if their already reduced role as parent may be further diminished or extinguished altogether. The risk is that their response will be to secure the children's loyalty by trying to undermine the children's relationship with the new partner.

If you are acting for the parent with care, it can be helpful to acknowledge how destructive that reaction is but also carefully point out the underlying anxiety which may be fuelling the behaviour. Recognising that the other parent feels dispossessed rather than in control can cushion the impact of the behaviour. It may allow your client to see that confrontation will only add fuel to an already brightly burning fire. Since the oxygen for the flames stems from the panic of loss you could suggest that the children are encouraged to make their love for the other parent very clear. Although that may seem a difficult thing to suggest to a client who is angry and upset by the other parent's activities, if the groundwork is done properly the suggestion may in fact be very well received.

Non resident parent

On the other hand, if you are acting for the other parent you can play an active role in providing reassurance about their continuing importance. You can emphasise that although it is helpful for children to be able to get along with new partners the natural parent has a unique place in their life.

A particularly difficult situation is when the new partner is perceived to have been a cause of the breakdown of the relationship. It may seem outrageous to the parent with care that their children may have to "be exposed" to the new partner. The children may themselves find that difficult to cope with. Younger children may find it acceptable so long as both their parents seem to approve older children may feel hurt and rejected.

Timing

The question of timing may be the key element in adapting to this change. Most parents with care, no matter how much they may protest, are likely to realise that the new partner will have to be involved in the contact arrangements at some point. It is crucial to avoid being too explicit about that immediately. It is entirely appropriate to acknowledge how difficult it is for not only your client but also the children to cope with all the changes. Emphasise how important it will be for the other parent to take that on board as well. Start exploring how the children could be helped to overcome their anxieties and worries about the separation.

At some point it should seem appropriate to recognise that part of the children's upset is the loss of the other parent. In working out how to minimise that loss it may become easier to think through arrangements which will allow the children to be part of the other parent's new life and to start gently probing about when that might involve the new partner. Emphasise this is not for the new partner's benefit nor indeed the other parent's but simply to allow the children a full involvement in the other parent's life. If your client remains intensely emphatic that the new partner must not be involved in the contact arrangements at any point on any condition it may be necessary to explore aloud what the other parent might do in response. Ask why the children would be at risk if they saw the new partner. Explain what would happen if things had to be sorted out in court. Point out that decisions would then be made by strangers rather than either parent. Ask the client their opinion of what a court might decide. Clients are often surprisingly judicial when invited to role play in this way! Let the client know the potential benefits of retaining control over the timing of any introduction.

The legal rules can often be used as a carrot rather than a stick.

Legal framework

One of the benefits of explaining the broad legal framework before going on to give specific advice is allowing the client space to absorb it as general information. Preface giving legal information by explaining that you thought it would be helpful if the client knew what you have to take into account in assessing the details they are providing. That creates a climate of information sharing. It puts a distance between you and the law. You can then more easily comment that some of the rules come as a surprise to many parents or may not be quite what parents expect. You can explain that the people who decide what the legal rules should be have taken into account what young people described as their experience of parental separation and what child care experts such as psychologists have said. You will not be seen as trying to "sell" the law to your client.

Most parents have some idea that the law relating to children involves both responsibilities and rights. They will rarely quarrel with the idea that decisions should be to benefit the children rather than the adults.

If the discussion has become sufficiently problem-solving it can be quite constructive to explore arrangements for the children from the perspective of sharing responsibility rather than dividing up rights. Working out how parents can share the load of childcare allows workable arrangements to emerge much more easily than dealing with the issue as a power struggle between the adults. Once the initial intensity fades most parents will accept that the more "taxi drivers" available in the lives of children the better!

It can also be helpful to point out that the starting point is an assumption that it will usually be better for parents to be able to make decisions about their own children. Involving the courts is seen as the last resort. Both parents lose control over the decision-making process.

It might also be worth looking ahead and recognising that a bitter struggle over arrangements at this stage is not going to resolve things once for all because of the changing needs of growing children and likelihood of changes in the adults lives as well.

Another aspect to dwell on is that while the practicalities of children's lives may be regulated by court orders the really significant aspect of the parent child relationship is the product of the interactions between parent and child which remains untouched by judicial decision.

In some cases a parent may be so engulfed by their own reaction to a separation that they lose sight completely of their children's needs. The formality of court procedure may help restore a more realistic perspective. In other cases children may unwittingly make each parent think that agreement between them is impossible.

Children's roles

Caretaker

Even quite young children will feel a tremendous sense of responsibility towards their parents after separation. They may worry about the sadness of the parent they are living with. They will be anxious about the practical arrangements of the other parent. They will be eager to reassure both parents and try to make them feel better. The sad aspect of this poignant concern is how often it leads to misunderstandings which increase rather than reduce conflict between the parents.

Children may return from a contact visit with only negative reports. In fact, they may have enjoyed their time with the other parent very much indeed but recognise a risk of this appearing disloyal. The underlying message may be that they love both parents very much. The immediate impact could be to suggest that contact is not working to their benefit.

A child might highlight deficiencies in the other parent's standard of living. This may come across as a "planted" complaint from the other parent but in reality be a spontaneous attempt by the child to elicit sympathy in the hope of reconciliation.

Reconciler

Children may tell each parent that they want to live with him or her. This can be a signal for a major dispute over residence when it really indicates a longing for both parents to be under the same roof.

Go between

One role that should never be imposed on children is that of "go-between". Sometimes parents will ask children to convey messages. They will explain how difficult it is for them to cope with the other parent's reaction to the content of such messages. It is very important for an advising lawyer to point out gently that if they as an adult have that difficulty it is not a responsibility which should be delegated to a child. This must be followed up by a discussion about how information can be conveyed by one parent to the other without involving the children.

Ally

Sometimes parents feel it necessary to justify their behaviour to their children or persuade the children that the other parent was at fault. Although it is important for children to have information about a separation their need is to know what implications the separation will have for them rather than to act as judge in respect of the adults. It diminishes children to have to work out if one or both parents is a "bad parent". It is better to let young people decide for themselves if and when they wish to sit in judgement of the parents. Both parents are likely to benefit in the long-term by avoiding explanations that really require an adult's maturity for understanding.

Children as individuals

It can be helpful at various stages to pause and ask for some detailed descriptions of the children involved in any dispute. Getting a client to paint a picture of each of the children can help the client focus on the children rather than on the adult dispute. It can reveal indications that a child or children may be struggling which could have implications about whatever course of action the client is considering. It could highlight that arrangements should be tailored more specifically for the needs of each child.

Sometimes hearing more about the children may reveal that a child's views may be in conflict with your client's instructions. You can then explain about the importance of taking into account children's views and see if some compromise could be made which could accommodate what both parent and child think important.

Obtaining quite detailed information can put a more practical slant on the discussion and lead into a more constructive approach.

In considering arrangements it is always important to check how realistic they are.

Reality testing

Although it is preferable to work towards a climate where parents will be able to communicate adequately about arrangements for their children if plans have to be made through legal advisers, it is essential to double check that they are workable. The detailed hand over arrangements must be discussed and set down if communication is difficult and times and dates must be completely clear. Any requests for changes in arrangements should give adequate time for instructions to be taken. A request by fax or e-mail on a Thursday afternoon for contact at the weekend is guaranteed to cause "contact rage" even if only between solicitors!

If parents are discussing quite complex arrangements for sharing the care of their children help them check the impact this may have on any out of school activities and to think out the implications for homework, school clothes and responsibility for dealing with notes from school.

Sometimes shared care arrangements work very well, sometimes they represent an unhappy compromise in power sharing between parents rather than the reflection of the importance of both parents to the children.

Strategies

If arrangements do seem fuelled by adult argument rather than co-operation it can be enough to discuss them in such detail that it becomes clear that the arrangement is unworkable and reveal the true difficulty which can then be tackled openly.

If one parent complains of the lack of "quality time" being spent by the other with the children it can be useful to ruminate on how relatively little face to face time parents in general do spend with their children. The benefit of a more natural "background" relationship could be discussed.

Sometimes the apparent problem is the refusal of a child to go with the other parent. If there are no serious failings on the part of the other parent which have been established it seems likely the source of the difficulty is the tension which has arisen at the point of handover. Exploring arrangements could avoid the parents being in direct contact and instead having a neutral person known to the child involved at hand over might be the best way forward. The use of a contact centre for a while might be another option.

If a history of violence is an issue then a similar arrangement, completely avoiding any contact between the parents and using a contact centre could allow the motivation of the other parent to be tested.

Conclusion

Try to help clients—

- Separate the role of parent from ex-partner
- See things from the child's perspective
- Take a long term view
- Be aware of other available resources

Further reading

Daniel Goleman, *Emotional Intelligence* (Bloomsbury)
   ISBN 0-7475-2830-6

Schaffer, *Making Decisions About Children*
   (2nd ed., Blackwell)
   ISBN 0-631-20259-5

Ann O'Quigley, *Listening to Children's Views* (Joseph
   Rowntree Foundation)
   ISBN 1-902-63370-9

Parkinson, *Family Mediation* (Sweet & Maxwell)
ISBN 0-421-58410-6

Rosemary Wells, *Helping Children Cope with Divorce*
(Sheldon Press)
ISBN 0-85969-777-0

CHAPTER 10

MEDIATION

"When one door opens another closes; but we often look so long and so regretfully upon the closed door that we do not see the ones which open for us."
Alexander Graham Bell

As discussed in Chapter 5, when touted as a universal panacea to all family law disputes or rejected outright as anathema, much unnecessary controversy is generated about mediation. When properly understood and employed as one of the range of options for resolving family disputes it is a valuable tool. All family law practitioners should understand the process and consider with their client, at the earliest stages, whether it is an appropriate way of resolving their problems.

Given the alternatives available, and with the knowledge of the likely financial and emotional cost of other options, a couple will often choose mediation as being the best route to a satisfactory conclusion.

What is mediation?

As mentioned in Chapter 5, this is a process where a couple with issues to resolve sit down with an impartial person, the mediator, to see if they can find a resolution. The mediator is there to assist the couple in the process. The couple emerge from mediation, if the process reaches a conclusion, with a set of proposals in a written document ("a summary of proposals") that they can take back to their independent solicitors for discussion. The aim for the mediator is to produce a summary that is easily understood by all concerned and can be quickly constituted as a binding contractual agreement.

The defining characteristic of mediation is that couples provide their own solutions. By taking responsibility for their problems and the solutions to them they are hopefully fixing the tone for the resolution of future difficulties. It is not uncommon for couples in dispute to reach an agreement through solicitors and then either explicitly or implicitly disown it, blaming the solicitor, a misunderstanding or outside pressure for what they perceive to be an unsatisfactory outcome. If a couple "own" a solution they may work harder to get it to succeed.

What is unique to mediation in the family law context is the management by the mediator of the two people in the same room. At the heart of the process is the modelling by the mediator of an alternative way of relating. For instance, by consistently bringing a couple back to an overarching shared mutual goal of achieving what is best for their children and away from the expression of individual adult preferences the aim is that, over time (and sometimes a dramatically short time), the couple will change the way they communicate and the values imbuing what they say. By presenting a couple with responsibility for decisions about their children inside mediation they can take and carry the same sense of responsibility into their future behaviour outside mediation. By fostering respectful communication and a better understanding of partners concerns in mediation ongoing relationships can be transformed.

Key elements of mediation

Non-binding

The proposals to emerge are not binding. The aim is to provide a check on a proposed outcome by ensuring each party gets independent advice on what they propose to do. Only after independent advice is obtained do the couple finalise a formal agreement.

Impartial facilitation not arbitration

One of the commonest misplaced expectations of mediation is that the mediator will arbitrate between a couple. This is not at all the case. The mediator is there, very specifically, to avoid the imposition of an outside solution (including by the mediator) to problems brought for discussion. The process works on the basis that the best solutions to our couple's problems come from the couple themselves working within the informed framework of the mediation.

Information not advice

The mediator can and should give legal information to the clients. A married couple who are separating need to have their discussions informed by a relevant understanding of the law. Solutions need to be related to legal principles and the detailed insight a couple have into their own needs and resources.

Confidential

Mediation is intended to be confidential other than in exceptional circumstances such as where a child is believed to be at risk. Factual information about financial matters is also given on an open basis.

Co-operation not opposition

By the very fact that they are at mediation it is obviously not possible for a couple to agree on what the detailed outcomes should be at the start of the mediation, however at a deeper level it is often possible for them to decide to approach things co-operatively and to identify common concerns—finding suitable accommodation, achieving what is best for the children, obtaining a fair division of assets. Mediation works from the assumption that, if people can be brought to see what they have in common, they will be more likely to reach agreement on how things should be resolved to provide for each of them. The aim is to promote co-operation, understanding, respect and full expression in finding solutions.

Future focus

Much time is spent in family law work identifying and setting out the history of a relationship. This is necessary, particularly in the context of court proceedings, because decisions are based on evidence of what has happened in the past as much as what is proposed for the future. This methodology is usually bad for ongoing relationships. One of the constants in literature about children following separation is the desirability of parents avoiding conflict over their children, focusing on the future and building on the positive elements in relationships (see Chapter 9). Court procedures require us to focus, in writing, on areas of conflict, to look back, and, to highlight the negatives in the other party's relationship with the children, which is exactly the opposite of what we are told children need. Mediation, by focusing on what will work for the future, hopes to foster a different way of talking.

Even where children are not involved, couples often want to move on without the wholesale contamination of memories of happier times by the vivid experience of current conflict. They may want to continue to see each other or at least to remain on speaking terms. Mediation can make that easier to achieve.

Voluntary

Either party can end mediation at any time they like. It is recognised that it is only possible to get someone to act cooperatively in a voluntary process. Involuntary cooperation is a contradiction in terms.

Openness

Parties are required to undertake to make a full disclosure of their financial circumstances. The parties are expected to be open about the facts, procedure and law. The intention is for decisions to be made with an awareness of the facts of a case, the parties respective interests and the legal principles looked to within the relevant jurisdiction in resolving those issues.

How mediation works

The stages

Agenda

The parties identify an agenda for what they want to discuss at the first meeting. They identify an order in which they want to deal with their agenda. They decide what information is needed and how it will be obtained. In identifying an agenda and deciding on how and what information to get the couple are assisted by the mediator giving legal and practical information as well as facilitating discussion.

Information gathering and presentation

Having ingathered information it is consolidated on a flipchart or in some other manageable form.

Options

From the information the parties progress to identifying what options are open to them to settle their dispute. Again the options are usually identified in a written form on a flip chart. It may be that the parties are certain what they want to do and it is clearly achievable provided a proper balancing of assets can be made. If that is the case the parties go straight ahead with the attempt to achieve that balance without identifying other options.

Choosing

If more than one option is identified more information may be required or, if not, the couple can proceed to consider whether each option can work in practice, in an attempt to "reality test" the possibilities. It is a matter of seeing whether the composite parts proposed for each party can coalesce into an affordable/practicable/fair solution. At this stage the advantages/disadvantages of particular proposals become evident and are flagged up. Finally the couple are assisted in moving towards a mutually acceptable joint proposal.

The Skills

A hugely important facet of mediation is the opportunity it gives a couple to treat their own situation as a set of mutual problems to be resolved not to battle to be fought out. Both "heart" and "head" need to be engaged. If the parties participation in the mediation process is infused with fear, anxiety, anger or all three, logic, analysis and problem solving will be displaced by confrontation and self protection.

The intention of a mediator is to create a relaxed informal open environment to make it easier for parties to talk about problems. The aim is to allow emotions to subside and a clear analysis to be made. Because of this most of the skills being used by the mediator, when used properly, should not be obvious and should be seamlessly integrated into the overall discussion. On the surface gliding effortlessly under the water paddling hard!

We have mentioned some of the techniques used earlier on this book because they are valuable skills outwith the mediation process. Acknowledging, normalising, reframing, forms of question, care in use of language, information gathering and giving, summarising and analysis—the mediator aims to use these skills, to model these new ways of relating, to foster positive and responsible attitudes while ensuring the parties are heard in a balanced way.

At its best, mediation can let people see that their story is not "either he is right or I am", an exclusive "either/or" battle, but rather a case of "I thought this but she thinks that and I can see that both can seem right to each of us", an inclusive "but / and" narrative.

Timescale

How long on the calendar the overall mediation process lasts largely depends on how often the couple and their mediator can meet and how quickly information can be put together. Each individual mediation session normally lasts about an hour and a half. How many mediation sessions are involved depends on the extent of the difficulties between the couple and the number and complexity of the issues. If no progress is made after four or five mediations both the couple and the mediator may be considering whether it is worth continuing. Broadly speaking a mediation running to a final set of proposals might be expected to last through three to nine sessions. However there are always the exceptions of the very simple or complex situation.

When is mediation particularly helpful/advantageous?

Some of the benefits of mediation have already been mentioned in Chapter 5. Many couples are determined to find their own solutions to the breakdown of their relationships, in particular where children are involved. Mediation gives an opportunity to do this in a structured way with skilled guidance. Given a joint exploration of the law, appropriate support in ingathering information and help in identifying options, a couple of this sort can identify the route that best satisfies their family's needs for the future in a fair and reasonable way, quite quickly.

Sometimes mediation is chosen where people are involved in considerable conflict. These people choose mediation precisely because other methods of resolution have failed and they do not want to pay for or rely on an imposed solution from the courts. In such cases a final set of proposals may not be reached but parties may emerge from the mediation with a better understanding of each other's position and gaps in those positions narrowed sufficiently to allow a successful negotiated settlement in a different forum. In other words mediation cannot be judged as a success or failure by whether a final all encompassing set of proposals emerges or not. As with other methods of resolution the costs and benefits can be difficult to measure. The improved understanding and communication obtained through a mediation terminated without "proposals" may still have made it a beneficial process.

Complex financial cases

Where there is a large amount of financial and other information to be in ingathered and discussed a couple can choose mediation as being an efficient method of identifying property and its value in a mutually acceptable way. The mediation might not go any further than that but would have still been a success if it achieved this desired goal.

Child related cases

The largest number of cases dealt with in mediation historically have been to do with children. The knowledge that children emerge best from separation when their parents can act cooperatively, when conflict is minimised and when their parents can give each other not just permission but "loving permission" to be with the children, is a powerful incentive to use mediation.

For a good decision to be made about children the most important element to be considered is likely to be the relationship the child has with each parent. That is often a matter of subtle shades and tone. Not a lot is learnt about these subtleties in the physically and emotionally buttoned up but charged atmosphere of court. Parents have the best information about the richness and texture, the emotional rapport between them and their children and other significant figures. That information can best be brought out and applied in mediation.

Children can be involved in the mediation with the agreement of the parties in a way appropriate to the particular case. If a couple can tap into their knowledge and understanding of their children in an honest way in mediation, that is a powerful motor towards appropriate practical solutions. What is even better is that the methodology of mediation gives a model for how future discussions about the welfare of the children could be discussed.

When is mediation unhelpful/inappropriate?

Mediators are trained to consider at the outset whether mediation may be inappropriate. By the outset we mean from the first telephone call onwards. For instance, if there are issues of violence, it may well be a case where mediation is inappropriate. Equally, where both parties are keen to mediate and the mediator is satisfied that sufficient safeguards are in place, a mediation could go forward. Each situation has to be weighed on its own merits.

Once a mediation is started it may become apparent that one party is unable to communicate or is refusing to communicate. There may be an obvious domination by one party or the other which is being continued in spite of the interventions of the mediator. In all these circumstances the mediator can decide that the case is not appropriate for mediation and end it.

Conclusion

We are back where we started. Not a universal panacea, but a powerful method of dispute resolution that, when used with the right people at the right time, can facilitate a significantly improved outcome to disputes for the whole family.

- Couples find their own solutions
- Non-binding
- Impartial facilitation not arbitration
- Co-operation
- Confidential
- Focus on the future
- Not always appropriate or helpful

CHAPTER 11

MANAGING A FAMILY LAW TEAM

*"Business is like a car: it will not run by itself except
downhill"*

American saying

Introduction

Your parallel objectives are to make the clients' interactions with
your office as positive as possible and to streamline the
administration of their work. "Front of House" activity should be
marked by courtesy, warmth and competence while the "engine
room" delivers efficient, prompt and effective service. Although
family lawyers need to be able to multi-task, you cannot achieve
all these objectives on your own. Every member of staff has the
potential to enhance or sabotage the firm's relationship with the
client. The more every employee can feel involved in the
importance of and satisfaction from helping clients the more the
staff are likely to enjoy their work and deliver an excellent service
to the clients.

If you are a partner you can use your interpersonal skills on
your colleagues to foster a co-operative working environment. If
you are an associate, assistant or trainee you can still use your
interpersonal skills to foster a co-operative working environment
though probably in a more oblique way. Use whichever of the
following suggestions that seem workable, adapted whenever
necessary.

Training

While every office will have its own structure, in most the key
colleagues for you will be the receptionist, your secretary and the
cashier. It helps a lot if you can set time aside to help those
members of staff develop appropriate skills. Most employees in
solicitors' offices are well motivated and responsible. They are
likely to have the potential and interest to extend their range given
support and encouragement to do so.

Staff meetings

Try to organise a regular meeting to allow discussion about work issues. The meetings need not take long but should involve all the members of staff who deal with your clients. Encourage suggestions about improvements which could be made. Foster the flow of information round the office. Get and give feedback about client reactions to the work. It's great to pass on the very welcome gratitude which comes our way. It's also important to explore why things go wrong.

Ground rules for training and staff meetings

The ground rules are to make it clear that the objectives for any staff training and staff meetings are to help staff enjoy their work to ensure that clients in turn enjoy dealing with your firm. Make it clear that the starting point is the assumption that everyone is trying to get it right and the recognition that things can still go wrong despite that. Staff meetings and staff training are not the place for rows.

Troubleshooting

When mistakes happen it is best to start by exploring how they happened with the individual staff members. Explain what you know of what happened and the consequences for the clients or the firm. Invite their explanation why things went wrong and their suggestions for how to put it right. Accept responsibility for any part you played. It can be constructive for the emphasis to be on how anyone who was responsible for a mistake might put things back on course. Any wider lessons can be fed into the staff meeting in a general, positive and non-attributable way.

It is very important to take appropriate steps when things do go wrong but equally important to do so in a problem-solving way. Most people feel bad about mistakes but if you pile on blame much of that feeling of responsibility will curdle into defensiveness.

Office practice manual

Use the office training as an opportunity to build up an office practice manual. Each member of staff can identify what tasks they perform and outline the key steps involved in each task. That can be used as a reference point and for new members of staff. It should be reviewed regularly and updated when there are any changes in the routine. It can be used to compile a skills inventory allowing each staff member to identify the range of skills they have. It helps members of staff have a better understanding of their colleagues' work. Building up an office practice manual can be done gradually using regular staff meetings or during the more extended periods for staff training. This approach can increase the likelihood of staff members being able to cover for colleagues at times of staff shortage. It could also highlight areas of office practice and procedure which have not quite been thought through.

If possible, provide some training input about non-legal aspects such as stress management, first aid and interpersonal skills.

Staff reviews

It is important to make time every so often to check how members of staff feel they are progressing. This can be done by way of a formal staff review perhaps annually. The risk is that such a review will acquire a rather daunting profile and in some offices may be linked with pay reviews. An alternative is to make the review more part of the ongoing training but in that case don't overlook regular individual meetings with staff members. Provide a clear structure. A combination of self-assessment of skills in relevant areas plus individual feedback from ongoing training can be useful. Always remember how important it is for people to feel appreciated.

Receptionist

The receptionist is indeed the most public face and voice of a business. Your receptionist can smooth ruffled feathers and often deal with practical queries which might otherwise have come your way. Remember that you can improve the receptionist's job satisfaction dramatically by getting your bit right. The most demoralising aspect of being a receptionist is dealing with disgruntled clients. Some steps you can take to minimise disgruntlement:

- Let the receptionist know when you'll be available so that if clients are asked to phone back they can be given a realistic time to try.

- Give your clients realistic estimates of the timescale for work you are doing for them. The receptionist tends to get the blame for the non-arrival of anticipated documents.

Security

It is important for the receptionist to be able to feel physically secure. Family law clients (and their former partners) can be very wired up. The layout of the office should be designed to provide appropriate distance and assistance if necessary.

Responsibility

Clients will press receptionists for advice and information. Help your receptionist to feel confident about identifying safe boundaries for what they can deal with and reliable procedures for passing on queries which lie outwith those boundaries.

Secretary

Legal secretaries can be invaluable colleagues, able to deal with a considerable amount on their own initiative. The key factors are training and supervision. It is essential to allow skills to develop at the right pace and monitor progress without being unduly restrictive. A useful and straightforward way of giving instruction is to explain more when you are doing dictation. Providing extra background information as you go along can be a rich source of training.

Review your secretary's skill base regularly. Check if they feel they would like to consider taking on the more responsibility for doing first drafts of documents for which there are set styles or templates. Remember that you are always responsible for the work produced! Don't be seduced by the gloss of professionalism applied by the printer. Check and double check.

Dictation

Be a good dictator! Speak clearly and avoid eating or drinking while dictating. Secretaries are admirable but should not expected to be telepathic or have more information about the client than you have.

Cashier

It can help enormously if everyone in the office understands something about the workings of the cash room and the reason for the need for accuracy. Maintaining a dialogue between the cash room and other members of staff can prevent unnecessary work for the cash room and needless mistakes. Most accounts systems will be computerised but the now rather mature adage "garbage in—garbage out" remains only too apt. Make sure your system encourages the provision of clear information to the finance department.

It does no harm to explain to staff members the very close link between your practising certificate and the correct running of the accounts department.

Office systems

It really is best (and possible) to be proactive rather than reactive in dealing with your workload. Nothing is going to make the work of a family lawyer easy but a systematic approach can make it manageable and enjoyable.

Every client provides a different challenge and opportunity in their particular circumstances and must always be recognised and treated as individuals. The paperwork associated with clients can, however, be streamlined since the paperless office remains on the horizon (though gaining focus) paper handling is still a feature!

File layout

This should be consistent for all solicitors engaged in family work and designed to make information accessible. It can be useful to keep the basic client information at the start of a file and updated as necessary. Filing must be up-to-date with any one day's notes and correspondence in time order. Make sure people do follow that protocol. It avoids heart-stopping moments on opening files to find an urgent message apparently never dealt with while it is a relief to excavate further and find a record of intense and appropriate activity. It is better to avoid those life- threatening moments.

Everyone dealing with client files should be quite clear about the system you adopt and the importance of following it. Files should be returned to where they are stored whenever not being actually worked on. It can be useful to have a system of coloured or labelled cards to be inserted in place of the files showing which member of staff is working on the file.

Filing Clerk

It is immensely valuable to have one member of staff who takes overall responsibility for the filing system. Remember that your filing system is the heart of an efficient office.

Accuracy

Remember and broadcast the carpenter's adage "Think twice, cut once!". If work is done correctly the first time, endless time and frustration is saved. This applies to us all; accuracy is essential in work ranging from framing a complex agreement to spelling a client's name correctly on a letter. In fact, misspelling a client's name can be a particularly public and upsetting mistake signalling a real lack of care to the client.

Delegation

Make sure that any regular and straightforward tasks are delegated. Develop office styles as templates which incorporate instructions to allow standard work to be carried out simply and accurately. Evolve routines. This is where training can be seen as a real investment. Well-trained staff can tackle a significant amount of the routine work at the first stage with sufficient supervision and checking and avoid you becoming a bottle neck. Once incoming mail is opened, a responsible member of staff can be appointed to sift this and e-mails, faxes and telephone messages, identify those which might be delegated and look out files for those which can't. You can check the sifting and allow the delegated tasks to be undertaken. Files for appointments should be looked out for you along with any files you have marked forward for checking. Your appointments diary can be kept by the receptionist who can then not only deal with making appointments but also keep an eye on how your day shaping up and be realistic about planning returned calls.

Work flow

Think of your work as incoming traffic! What you want is a system with clear sign posts for work which can be sent off immediately towards another member of staff where that is an appropriate destination. Work will need to "drive past" you but if it is immediately clear where it should be heading, send it there at once. If more complex directions are needed "park" the work out of the traffic flow but not out of mind until you can deal with it. Remember to deal with the "parked" tasks—over staying can involve ferocious penalties!

Apply the same approach to your desk. Let the work flow on, through and off. Have clearly designated parking spaces for different categories of traffic—incoming, telephone calls, drafting, thinking and outgoing spaces could be useful. Have proper spaces for incoming and outgoing bits of paper, separate from files, to stop preventable accidents.

Have sufficient space for incoming non-client traffic which may be needed in the future. It can be useful to have "multi-storey car parks" for broad categories of information is so you do not need to give too much attention or mental energy to categorise it. A concertina file or big ring binder could be an appropriate destination.

The key thing is to keep the traffic flowing—deal with any incoming traffic immediately either by sending on to its next destination at once by delegation or dictation or by "parking" it appropriately, either a long or short stay. Use gaps in the traffic of work to do with some of the short stay "parked" stuff. Set aside predictable "off peak" times to deal with some of the "long stay" stuff and if that park is getting full or overdue, divert the rest of the traffic so you can deal with it. Just keep it all moving!

Time management

Give your working days, weeks and months a clear structure. Have time marked out in the diary to deal with incoming mail, a slot for telephone calls, preferably morning and afternoon and for checking and signing mail.

Build in time free from appointments to deal with the paperwork which will accumulate (and use it for that—not to read some periodical which suddenly seems irresistibly interesting but make sure you pencil in opportunities to catch up with reading as well). Recognise what time of day you can concentrate best and use that to tackle the more demanding paperwork. Specifically diary time-consuming tasks rather than keeping files lurking reproachfully on your desk. After you see a client whenever possible deal with any dictation arising immediately. If you can see the work will take longer than the time available then be realistic about how much time is necessary. Where there might be an opportunity of dealing with the work later in the day then put the file in the "short stay" pile. If the work involved is likely to take a while consider giving it an "appointment" for later and put the file away until then.

Try to avoid files piling up on your desk. If there is a pile of accumulated files at the beginning of your day look at each one and put in order of priority. Have a "hot spot" on your desk for matters you must deal with that day (and make sure you do!)

Have a planner to mark "away fixtures" on. Keep court commitments very visible. Make sure your diary systems are carefully thought through to deal with appointments, forward tasks and court commitments. Forward court dates are one aspect of office life which can bear duplication. Build a regular file check into your system. Checking a few files once a week is a lot less daunting than a monthly wrestle with your entire client base! Diary files forward when sending out letters with either an implicit or explicit time limit.

Technology

Make as much use of technology as possible. If you are working in an office where you have your own computer terminal it would help to have the directory system set up to make it easy to access the client's work. You could then call up outgoing letters when clients phone to discuss them. You could dictate the letters setting out the points to be discussed and your preliminary thoughts in a way which will make it all the easier to deal with the discussion without the need for the file. By doing this, you may well create a letter that will be more understandable to the client by setting out more fully in the letter the background, issues and options than you might otherwise have done. If an incoming letter raises issues you have already discussed to some extent with your client you could do a draft response and send it out with a copy of the letter for the client's instructions. E-mails can come to you direct and avoid the frustration of endless missed telephone calls. Voice mail can also be useful to allow continuing communication in your absence although that does lose the opportunity of other members of staff helping. Internal e-mails can avoid the need for some meetings and focus the ground to cover when they are necessary. A networked diary system and database is a great way of allowing shared information to be kept up to date and accessible within the office. An interesting web site performs the same function for the public face of the office.

Use office standard documents to draft client work. The ability to use a spreadsheet should cut down the frustration otherwise involved of assembling and updating financial information.

Just try to avoid inadvertently holding on to work which could be efficiently tackled by your receptionist or secretary.

An absolute necessity is to have an utterly dependable backup system to ensure that all the information on computer is copied very regularly. The current backup should be kept outwith the office.

Although an energetic approach to office systems can make work more enjoyable there are pitfalls other than overwork to avoid.

Professional issues

Conflict of interests

Remember the importance of having systems in place to prevent taking on clients when a conflict of interest could arise. This can be surprisingly difficult because of the endless succession of addresses and surnames which clients often inhabit. Use computer search facilities to make this easier.

Security

You should be aware of security issues for yourself as well as other members of staff. It's really not advisable to see clients after hours if no other members of staff are around. Have a "panic button" or alarm system. Be very alert to client security also. Ensure all office staff are absolutely clear of the importance of not revealing whether or not any individual is a client of your firm to any enquirer (unless authorised to do so). It is important to talk through with staff how any such enquiries should be handled especially if you dealt with clients whose activities may be of interest to the media or their ex-partner.

Skeletons

Family law work makes demands on your heart and head! Inevitably, there will be cases which worry you for one reason or another. Make sure you have a routine where you and a colleague can discuss difficult cases. It is worth making such an exchange a relatively formal occasion. Think over your problem case or cases before the meeting. Be able to concisely summarise the difficulty for your colleague. Approach the exchange on the basis that each of you should ask one another helpful questions in the main rather than provide answers. Being asked relevant questions about what you have done or could do can be a very powerful way of tackling problems.

Credit control

As well as always maintaining the focus on client and job satisfaction it's worth helping other staff members understand the necessary relationship between chargeable time, efficiency and the profitability of the firm. Awareness of the rather narrow margin in family law work can prevent steps being overlooked and generate a more integrated approach.

Conclusion

- Promote teamwork and understanding of objectives
- Recognise the benefit of training and communication
- Keep the work flowing!

CHAPTER 12

YOUR SURVIVAL!

"If the stone falls on the egg – alas for the egg.
If the egg falls on the stone alas for the egg."
(Greek Cypriot proverb)

Difficult situations

People often express admiration for family lawyers on the basis
that we must have to deal with "awful people" in the mess of
personal relationships. Naturally we do deserve admiration!
Probably not for this reason. The truth of the matter is that family
law clients are no different from other people. In the context of
your work you will see the full range of human behaviour you
might expect in crisis—from the dignified, unselfish, and noble to
the downright petty, selfish, and deceitful. We are all capable of
exhibiting these ranges of behaviour in the right, (or wrong)
circumstances. Family breakdown is certainly a potent set of
circumstances and the negative behaviour we see often stems
from those circumstances.

The fact that we understand why people behave in a particular
way does not necessarily make it any easier to cope with. As we
said at the beginning of this book you, as much as your client, are
entitled to respect and fair treatment. If a client is not prepared to
afford you these things you should not feel obliged to act for
them. There are some people who are so aggressive and
unreasonable with you that you should stop acting (but do
consider whether there are mental health issues behind the
behaviour). There are other people who are difficult but
manageable. It is with this category that we can offer some help.

The low self-esteem client

New solicitors are usually advised to guard against the easy
generalisation and yet there is one trait that you will almost
invariably see in the newly separated client, low self-esteem. The
failure of a long-term relationship is usually perceived by both
parties as a failure by each of them as an individual. The

breakdown of the relationship has often been preceded by a history of negative comments, argument, abuse or even violence. The more difficult the history the more self-confidence tends to suffer. One of the ways we react to a loss of confidence is with a fear of decisions and a belief that we are destined to fail.

If a client expresses a sense of helplessness it is useful to let them know that this is a normal and understandable reaction to their situation. It is important to be positive and let them know that you have seen many people with similar feelings who have moved on to a different, but nonetheless satisfactory, life.

Arthur Koestler in his collection of essays "The Yogi and the Commissar" refers to the conundrum we all face in the internal battle between our sense of the vast deterministic forces apparently shaping our lives set against our own free will. He gives the example of the temptation to on drinking and to have a meal rather than sit down and write an essay. At one level he believes that his actions are predetermined. He finally persuades himself to sit down and write the essay. He feels very satisfied with himself.

> "From a scientific point of view this satisfaction is entirely spurious, since the issue was already settled before I started fighting myself; it was also settled that I should feel this spurious satisfaction and write what I write. Of course in my heart of hearts I do not believe that this is so, and I certainly did not believe it a quarter of an hour ago. Had I believed it, the process which I call "inner struggle" would not have taken place, and fatality would have served me as a perfect excuse for going on drinking. Thus my disbelief in determinism must be contained in the set of factors which determine my behaviour; one of the conditions for fulfilling the prearranged pattern is that I should not believe that it is prearranged."

The philosophical ponderings of Koestler may seem a long way from the needs of the family law client and yet the lesson arrived at is an important one. If you feed your client fatalistic renderings of the facts and the future and your client buys into your fatalism then the foundations for a self-fulfilling negative outcome are laid (a kind of negative placebo effect). There is no credit in foisting an entirely personal negative world view on an individual in a difficult situation. A positive future focus with a vision of your client in control of his or her destiny provides an entirely different aspiration which may well be attained (we're not talking "Pollyanna" here just a focus on the stars rather than the gutter!). The model comes from you.

In the relatively recent past and still today solicitors have taken on the role of paternal adviser or liberal combatant of the clients cause with the client as passive, almost helpless, bystander. This was and is a way of advising guaranteed to reinforce the individuals fatalistic passivity. We have advocated a positive involvement of the client in decisions not only because the client is best equipped to find the solution that suits them but also because the client is then better equipped to meet the future.

As with other areas there are shades to what we say. There are individuals who do not have the intellectual or emotional wherewithal to take up all the strings. We accept that in such circumstances an advisory solicitor has to be more forceful in highlighting the benefits or disadvantages of a particular choice.

It is important to stress that empowering the client does not mean abdicating our role as adviser and, where necessary, assertive combatant. It does mean that, in deciding the future course of an individual's family or independent life, where possible he or she should pull the strings.

The drifter

Many clients feel unable to take their situation forward often for long periods of time. The whole matter may be so painful and full of anxiety to them that they would rather do nothing than face it. This is a difficult one for you. On one hand you have to respect your client feelings and instructions, on the other hand your view may be that the unresolved business gives every appearance of being a continuing sore in the life of your client. As with many of these situations sympathetic honesty is usually the best starting point for deciding what do. Put your concern to your client. He or she may well be aware of the tension him or herself your comment may be the catalyst for an honest examination of motives and decisive in bringing your client to act. That is fine. It is also fine if your client indicates that he or she still does not what do anything. The choice is always the clients. The important thing is that they have an insight into the reasons for their choice.

If a client is swithering then things that can help are an objective examination of what is involved. Is it really terrifying to ingather the financial information? Is it really terrifying to have to visit a court for one day in time to narrate why a relationship went wrong? What is behind the fear? The anxiety may simply be firmly attached to the words "divorce", "court appearance". The anxiety may disappear if those things are discussed in their component parts and the client encouraged to deal with things a step at a time.

A second useful strategy is to set out a joint plan with timescales and review dates. It is nearly always more manageable for client to have a bit of paper setting out a plan with timing of individual elements than to contemplate an indefinite series of points for resolution with no clear idea or plan of how they are to be resolved

What is important is that you do not just accept the status quo yourself. One of the easiest traps to fall into as a family lawyer is that of mirroring in your approach the attitude of your client. If the client is inactive you need to be proactive in establishing the reasons for that inactivity at appropriate moments in your management of the case. You can give your client an insight into the reasons for inactivity and the pros and cons of that inactivity and help him or her decide whether to continue in that vein or not.

The hyperactive client

Particularly at the earliest age of the breakdown of relationships clients can express their anxiety by a constant barrage of activity. That is fine if the activity is purposeful and useful. In the legal context the danger is that the activity will not only be purposeless and useless but potentially damaging to the clients long-term interests.

A very angry client may want to dash into court to "take him for everything he's got", to "expose her adultery". The desire is understandable. The job of you as adviser is to acknowledge the emotion behind the attitude and to explore how the proposed course of action would advance your client's interests. It is an opportunity to explain the law does not operate as an instrument of retribution in family law cases. It is usually helpful to give your client an insight into the normal range of emotional reactions to separation—anger, sadness, bitterness acceptance. More importantly you can explain that the initial emotions can change and that it is normal to experience any one or all of these emotions in any one minute, week, year, lifetime following a separation. If emotions are so changeable it is normally not wise to make an irrevocable decision in the first days the client is experiencing these emotions (again situations of danger for the client, concern for children, can be exceptions to this). "Take your time" is a useful admonition. We have both seen relationships set of on an unremitting downward spiral following correspondence sent or proceedings taken, in justified anger. The problem is that the end of that spiral, however justified, may not ultimately be wanted. You are the still, quiet voice of calm not the "avenging angel"!

Hyperactivity can take other forms, some of which is are covered in later categories in this chapter. A natural response to anxiety is to try and cover all possibilities for the future. The "what ifs" that can wake us all up too early in the morning. There is difficult balance to be achieved here. On one hand reassurance needs to be given. On the other hand the exploration of endless speculative hypotheses certainly takes time, and therefore money, it can engender considerable unnecessary anxiety.

There are two ways to deal with these "what ifs". One is to give the client a kind of "hierarchy of likeliness". If something is likely to happen it may be worth exploring as a hypothesis to see how it would fit for the client. That goes at the top of the hierarchy. The lower you go in the hierarchy the less likely the thing is to happen and the more sense there is in "sticking it to the wall" or agreeing to "cross the bridge when we come to it". The second way is to simply cross all bridges as you come to them and not before. You would, for instance, have no hypothesising about what would happen if your client were to keep the family home and take on the mortgage until you have confirmed the building society or bank would allow it. The reasoning is that with every step along the path the direction of the next step becomes clearer. The best decisions are made with the fullest information and client can save time and money by waiting until the relevant information is to hand before looking at how options might work.

The highs/lows client

Naturally in the emotional river of family crises there are clients who surge through emotional rapids then float into a counter-flowing eddy of uninterest. This is the client who tells you one day he wants to go the "whole way" and the next day he just "wants out of it". It is important to address this syndrome directly with the client. A case of honesty being, once again, the best policy. You have to point out the difficulty for you in presenting a consistent approach to the other side, the danger that the day on which a deal is done is a day your client is in the wrong frame of mind. You have to help your client to a true sense of what he or she wants to do. You are assisted by bringing them back to the legislative emphasis on fairness and non retribution.

Where a client is changeable remember to confirm the problem and the tenor of ongoing discussions and instructions in writing. It gives you protection and your client a history of the effect of his indecision.

The talker

Some clients would like to speak to you every day for at least an hour. To some extent that is their prerogative if they pay for it. However it is usually undesirable. Mentioning that it is actually "dear to talk" can curtail unnecessary talk. A renewed explanation of the limits of your role can also be expedient.

The above is all fine and good but there is still the irrational, compulsive talker on the phone who wants you as his or her therapist regardless. Sometimes you have to be a wee bit "tough". As a, close to, last resort it can be beneficial to ask your client, very directly, what relevance a particular line of talk has to their case. As it has no relevance you are then in a position to point that out and hopefully end the conversation or guide it back onto a more constructive path. Closed questions can also assist you. If you ask "how did contact go?" When the only live issue is whether mum arrived at the right place at the right time to collect junior you are inviting a glorious Technicolor narration. If you ask "did your ex-partner arrive at the Post Office at 5p.m.?" You will get the information you need and then be able to weigh up whether any thing else of significance needs to be explored.

Another important element in closing down the conversation is your choice of words/sounds and tone of voice. If you are a liberal user of "Mmm I see" you will have lots of very long telephone conversations. If you are a master of the timed intervention "right, I see, that's interesting Mr Jones, let me ask you this" (followed by specific closed questions) or "right, thank you, Mr Jones, I will bear that in mind, what I am going to do is…. we can discuss any other points when we next meet, thank you for your call" you are giving yourself a better chance of exiting sane and with your client feathers relatively unruffled.

The best way out of all, of course, is if you can get away with "I know you are very busy, I will let you get away now. Thank you for your call." You have ended the conversation and your client feels you have ended the conversion to help them!

As with all the other categories sympathetic honesty can be the best tactic of all. Express your concern to do the best you can for your client and the fact that in order to do that you want to keep them to the relevant information. You are not getting relevant information at present, could you ask them a few questions. If you can get in control of the conversation you are a long way towards sorting the difficulty out.

The silent client

In some ways silence can be just as difficult to manage as talk. Be prepared to ask a question and wait until you get an answer. Be prepared to ask and return to very specific questions if you need information or answers. Consider whether your client may be suffering from depression or a related condition.

If you are having difficulty helping because of the detachment of your client say so.

The aggressive client

This can be the most difficult one of all. People under stress can direct their feelings of frustration and hostility towards you. If this persists after you have acknowledged their feelings appropriately, you may have to point out to your client that he or she is directing his or her anger towards you. That is often enough to stop the problem.

If honesty does not work you have to be firm. Family work is difficult enough without having to deal with persistent aggressive behaviour. Advise your client, verbally first, and then, if necessary, in writing that their behaviour is not acceptable and will lead to you withdrawing from acting if repeated. If that does not work stop acting well before you get to a crucial date when your client's position may be prejudiced by you withdrawing from acting.

We have known solicitors who have continued to act for clients because they were terrified of them. You should never get into that position. If an incident of aggression is serious enough, on any occasion, including the first, you should feel able to withdraw. If you do not delineate appropriate boundaries to behaviour you are tacitly giving the message aggressive behaviour is acceptable. The acceptance can have repercussions in directions well beyond your professional practice.

The passive client

This is the client who is determined to avoid any disagreement. We can applaud conciliatory approaches to family law problems but what is perceived as constructive conciliation can actually be or become questionable acquiescence. As with other situations it is a question of interpretation and balance as to where the line is drawn. Much of what we have said about the low self esteem client applies here. It is important to establish the reason for the passivity. If, after you have used your people skills to the full, your client is determined to follow a path outwith the range of what would be considered under the law you should make sure they know it and put your views in writing. If the client insists on acquiescence you have to follow their instructions. If you are wholly uncomfortable with those instructions you have the option of withdrawing from acting.

The over-friendly client

You may take the view that there can be no such thing as an over-friendly client. Certainly a friendly relationship is highly desirable and is part of the sympathetic rapport you want to achieve. However where a client establishes a very close relationship it can be difficult to be objective and give advice the client might not want to hear. If the professional relationship turned sour it can be particularly awkward. It is often the most informal client who can become the most aggressive complainer if things go wrong. Be careful to maintain your sympathetic but professional approach and be prepared to remind your client of the nature of your role in their affairs.

The bad file

This is the file we cannot face for some inexplicable reason. It lies festering in the recesses of our filing cabinet. There usually is no real problem in the file but you yourself can rapidly become the problem. Some offices have a system of allowing the rotation of a set number of files periodically, handling the transition carefully for the client. Your bad file is handed on to someone who can take a fresh look at it and move things forward. Whether it is informal or otherwise a system to allow this to happen is a good thing. If you have to stick with it a thorough review of the file with a note of its history and action points can help to overcome a block.

How to survive

Over the years lawyers have been one of the easiest targets for the humorist. Jokes abound telling a receptive public about the greedy, unscrupulous people lawyers are. It is rarely possible to relate them to the work we do. Dealing with people at moments of high conflict is no joke and the pressures created can be enormous. Greed and unscrupulousness are not easy to get on to the agenda! The themes developed in this book are not intended to put more pressure on you or to create a new set of stresses which you feel obliged to meet. We hope that an explanation of skills and practice will make your job easier.

It may seem strange to have a section on your survival needs but we believe that unrealistic expectations placed on you by yourself, your employers, your clients, or all three can be endlessly destructive to you, your employers and your clients. Stress is to be expected as part of most jobs but it has to be kept under control and minimised as for far as possible. We offer our views on self-preservation in the knowledge that everyone has to find strategies that work for them.

We are all infinitely fallible

When you start out in practice in there is an assumption that somewhere out there is the true "professional", the person who has every possible attribute and skill needed for the job. It normally takes a few years (or a few days depending on how cynical you are) to realise that person does not exist. Even the best lawyers make mistakes and have weaknesses. Certainly always aspire to do better but do not make the mistake of thinking that you will always do the best. If you create impossible expectations of yourself, rather like the Greek Cypriot egg in the opening quotation, you will always end up broken. Do not be complacent, but be kind to yourself!

We are not built to work 24 hours a day

This may come as a surprise to you! Legal aid rates paid to family lawyers often make us feel as though we need to run twice as fast to arrive at the same place as our privately paid colleagues. The reason it makes us feel like this is because it is true. Legal aid rates are substantially lower than recommended private rates. You may consider this indefensible but that does not make it any easier to bear. Points to remember are:

- If money is your main motivation consider carefully whether you want to be a family lawyer!
- If your employers want you to do only legal aid work they have to have a realistic expectation of what financial return is achievable. If necessary be prepared to set out the mathematical facts about what is possible in a working day. (If you have done the calculation start adjusting your financial expectations now!)
- If you are self-employed what applies to an employee applies to you.

This is not to say that you cannot make a living as a family law practitioner. It does mean that it is more difficult and requires you to work at the maximum of your efficiency.

If you do private work you can still face unrealistic demands. There are many family lawyers who have lost their health and /or their will to work in the field by demanding too much of themselves. Remember:

- Your health does come first.
- You need rest and recreation like any other human being.
- Money can buy many things but at some point there is a substantially diminishing return when you measure material pleasures gained against personal costs incurred. Do not sacrifice your happiness, or that of those around you at home and at work, to meet penal financial goals.

It is easy to say these things in a book and much more difficult to carry them into the workplace. However if you are going to do this work for the long-term a balance needs to be found.

Monitor and regulate how you work

The study of ergonomics is a well-established part of management practice. It makes sense to consider whether your files/desk/room/office are laid out to maximise your efficiency and comfort. If not ensure that things are changed as far as possible so that they are.

If you are working long hours and generating fees that suggest a relatively small number of chargeable hours are being achieved and have no good explanation for the discrepancy see where the chargeable hours are lost by time recording your working day. (The benefits of this self-study can be immediate and long-term!)

A change in the way you organise yourself, even by such a simple thing as for instance putting fee notes on a different colour paper from the rest of your file, can save you time and stress over and over again.

Water under the bridge is water under the bridge

If you have made a mistake take the lesson from a mistake and move on. We have all made the staggeringly daft comment in court or elsewhere. A certain solicitor close to this pen maintained in a long argument on the phone with another solicitor that there were 352 days in a year not 365! We have all sent a letter to the wrong address. Do not relive your bad moments in a pointless wallow in the past.

Achieve a sympathetic rapport not empathetic identification with your clients

For a lot of family lawyers this is the most difficult balance to achieve and the greatest source of stress. It is perfectly natural to be engaged by the story a client tells us and to want to help them. Helping them is one of the satisfactions of the job. The difficulty comes when that engagement tips over into actual identification with the client. You can become consumed with anxiety at the prospect of your client losing the children, the house, the money. Even when your client has insisted on pursuing an unrealistic goal you take their failure to get it as a personal disaster. You move from taking a proper pride in doing your job to the best of your ability into a sense of failure if a sheriff does not see things your way or a settlement does not get your client what he or she wants.

Once again it is easy enough to talk about this difficulty but much more challenging to sort it out. The only answer is to check through your own thinking to see what an anxiety or concern is based on. If it is based on a belief that you are not doing your job properly that is okay provided you address it, move on (and remember your fallibility!). If it is based on the fact that your client may not get what he or she wants, provided you have advised him or her of your view of the likelihood of success, you may well be over identifying with your client. You can hope that doing your job will mean getting what your client wants on many occasions but, by definition, there is a solicitor on the other side of the case with similar motivations whose client wants something else. Do not attach your self-esteem to the success or failure of your clients.

Give and get peer support

This is no doubt something we often do without thinking about it. It is nonetheless valuable for that. The best way to relieve your anxiety is often to share it and to know that other people have similar anxieties. The only people who can fully understand the pressures you cope with are others doing the same thing.

There is nothing wrong with having a more formal support arrangement. Regular case conferences or specific times available each week for discussion can be helpful. The important thing is to have some mechanism.

Humour

One of the best ways of keeping things in perspective is to have a good appreciation of the funny side of what we do.

Read about it!

There are books about how to draft writs, conduct a proof and the like. If you are concerned about these things check your understanding against a source such as a book.

Where interpersonal skills are concerned we hope this book can be one of your sources. It no doubt has its imperfections, things you would do differently, but if it gives you a first map, a starting point for your own revisals and development then it will have been worth writing.

Above all, remember that if you do use your skills and information constructively and realistically you will find yourself enjoying your work!

Conclusion

- Identify what makes a client difficult and find a strategy to address that difficulty
- Do not ignore it
- Admit "bad files" exist and have a strategy to deal with them
- We are all infinitely fallible
- You are not built to work 24 hours a day
- Have a sympathetic rapport not an empathetic identification with your client
- Give and get peer and other support.

INDEX